Leading Change
in Health Care
Building a Viable System
for Today and Tomorrow

IAN MORRISON

D1564843

press

HEALTH FORUM, INC.
An American Hospital Association Company
Chicago

ISBN: 978-1-55648-383-7   Item Number: 108107

PROJECT MANAGER: Joyce Dunne
EDITORIAL ASSISTANT: Barbara Novosel
LAYOUT AND TYPESETTING: Fine Print, Ltd.
COVER DESIGN: Cheri Kusek
PRODUCTION MANAGER: Martin Weitzel
ACQUISITIONS AND DEVELOPMENT: Richard Hill

Library of Congress Cataloging-in-Publication Data
Morrison, J. Ian.
   Leading change in health care : building a viable system for today and tomorrow / Ian Morrison.
      p. cm.
   Includes index.
   ISBN 978-1-55648-383-7 (alk. paper)
1. Medical care—United States—Forecasting. 2. Leadership. I. Title.
   RA395.A3M676 2011
   362.10973—dc22
                                                          2011011340

To Nora,
who read every word before anyone else did,
and who helped shape what you read here

Contents

On the building blocks of health reform

On politics and policy in the moment— a window on the time

On structural change

On lessons from abroad

On leading and legislating

On securing our future

About the Author

Ian Morrison is an internationally known author, consultant, and futurist specializing in long-term forecasting and planning, with a particular emphasis on health care and the changing business environment. He combines research and consulting skills with an incisive Scottish wit to help public and private organizations plan their longer-term future.

Morrison has written, lectured, and consulted on a wide variety of forecasting, strategy, and health care topics for government, industry, and nonprofit organizations in North America, Europe, and Asia. He has spoken to a wide range of audiences, from the boards of *Fortune* 100 companies to the Chinese Academy of Social Sciences in Beijing. He has worked with more than one hundred *Fortune* 500 companies in health care, manufacturing, information technology, and financial services. He is a frequent commentator on the future for television, radio, and the print media.

Morrison is the author of *Healthcare in the New Millennium: Vision, Values and Leadership* (Jossey-Bass, 2002). His previous book, *The Second Curve: Managing the Velocity of Change* (Ballantine, 1996), was a *New York Times* Business Bestseller and a *Businessweek* Bestseller. He has co-authored several books and chapters, including *Future Tense: The Business Realities of the Next Ten Years* (William Morrow, 1994) and *Looking Ahead at American Health Care* (McGraw-Hill, 1988). He also has co-authored numerous articles for publications such as *Chief Executive, Encyclopaedia Britannica, Across the Board, The British Medical Journal, The New England Journal of Medicine,* and *Health Affairs.*

Morrison is president emeritus of the Institute for the Future (IFTF). He is a founding partner in Strategic Health Perspectives, a joint venture between Harris Interactive and the Harvard School of Public Health's Department of Health Policy and Management. From 1996 to 1999, Morrison was retained by Accenture (formerly Andersen Consulting) as chairman of the Health Futures Forum. In that capacity, he chaired a number of international forums on the future of health care.

Before coming to IFTF in 1985, Morrison spent seven years in British Columbia, Canada, in a variety of research, teaching, and consulting positions. He holds an interdisciplinary PhD in urban studies from the University of British Columbia; an MA in geography from the University of Edinburgh, Scotland; and a graduate degree in urban planning from the University of Newcastle-upon-Tyne, England. He is a member of the board of directors of SFN Group (an NYSE company); a past director of the Health Research and Educational Trust (HRET), the research and education arm of the American Hospital Association; a director and current chair of the California Health Care Foundation; and a past director of the Center for Health Design. Morrison also serves as a member of the Stakeholders Advisory Committee of the Program on Health System Improvement at Harvard University.

Preface

This volume represents a collection of short essays written over almost a decade for Health Forum—a company that is owned by the American Hospital Association (AHA) and that publishes *Hospitals & Health Networks (H&HN)* magazine and its online editions, *H&HN Weekly* and *H&HN Daily*. Rick Hill, the editor of *H&HN Weekly* and the editorial director of AHA Press, approached me with the idea of publishing a volume that would include a selection of these essays for use by hospital leaders in board and leadership education.

I am incredibly flattered that these periodic missives might be deemed useful. I am incredibly excited by the prospect of having them published in one place in a way that makes them portable and accessible for leaders. (Maybe there is an app for that, too.) But also, as I reread, updated, and reflected on this collection, I saw that there were some important, overarching themes that Rick (as editor) and I (as columnist) had identified and explored and that, as a collection, these columns tell an important story.

It goes like this.

Leaders have to look ahead and make judgments about the future even though the future is highly uncertain. While no one, not even futurists, can truly predict its exact course, leaders need help in thinking systematically about the future.

Health care is large, complex, and expensive, but fundamentally it is about providing health and health care services to patients in a way that is compassionate, of high quality, and cost-effective.

How we organize and pay for health care in a way that is compatible with American values is a challenge because we, as a society, believe in choice, competition, consumerism, and cost sharing much more than do the peoples of any other country. It is difficult in the American context to find the correct balance between government and the market, between the role of organizations and the individual, and between information and incentives. But no matter what happens, the health care system will be subjected to ever more sophisticated scrutiny in the future, and the results will be shared transparently with patients, providers, and policymakers alike. Leaders will be held accountable for achieving higher performance.

Over the last decade, a health reform debate was building in this country that came to a head in the historic passage of the Patient Protection and Affordable Care Act (PPACA) in March 2010. The reform (with all its flaws) was constructed on a series of building blocks and compromises that reflected the unique politics and policy of the time. The act is a larger, more grandiose form of the Massachusetts Health Care Reform Plan and similar policy proposals made in California—created by Republican governors in strongly Democratic states. A series of essays explores the building blocks of health reform, in particular some key elements of who pays—and how—for the expanded coverage enacted in PPACA.

The story of reform was not without its twists and turns and was shaped, and will continue to be shaped, by big shifts in politics and the economy. To provide a window on those key turning points, five essays are republished here exactly as they were written at the time. (The essays appear under the heading "On politics and policy in the moment—a window on the time," pp. 87–107.)

- The first essay, written in the summer of 2004 before President George Bush was re-elected, looks ahead to the 2008 presidential election as the critical health care election. It proved to be that, just as elections yet to come will prove to be critical to health care.
- The second essay, written on the eve of the 2008 presidential primaries, argues for health reform that addresses the issues of affordability, quality, and sustainability in addition to coverage expansion. Reform that only addresses the latter misses an opportunity to transform health care, to deliver much higher performance, for decades to come.
- The third essay was written in December 2008 in the depth of the economic meltdown—a perilous time for the global economy, at

the bottom of a recession that would prove to have long-lasting effects on health care.

- The fourth essay, written the day President Barack Obama was inaugurated in January 2009, reflects on his re-election prospects and how health care will be critical to how his presidency is judged.
- The fifth essay, written in the fall of 2009, describes the extreme partisan acrimony and lack of true dialogue at the height of the health reform debate—making fun, it is hoped, of both sides in a fair and balanced way.

Overall, the basic message of this entire volume is that we need structural change in the way we deliver and finance health care so that it is more affordable and of higher quality for all Americans. Achieving this goal will require health care leaders to transform their organizations for higher performance. It is hard, but important, work. We can learn from each other, and we can learn from abroad (although no single health system has all the answers).

We can secure a better future with good leadership, great strategic thinking, and excellence in execution. Managing the roller coaster of change in policy and the economy can be done. It must be done.

Good luck with the future. It is in your hands.

Ian Morrison
Menlo Park, California
February 2011

Leading Change
in Health Care

On thinking about the future

The Median and the Edge

*We need to distinguish
between the future that's arrived
and the future that may never come.*

We often compress the future. We look ahead, see a large, inevitable future, and presume it is close. I have called this *premature extrapolation*. It is part of a larger problem in long-term forecasting and strategy development: We lack discipline even about the emerging reality. More specifically, we fail to distinguish between the median (the mainstream or the norm) and the edge (the 3 percent early adopters, leaders, harbingers, or just plain flakes who may or may not become the median of the future).

You see it in corporate strategy: Early adopters are assumed to be mainstream, and corporate bets are made as if those early adopters represent the norm. The new, new thing takes on an air of inevitability as the mainstream, even though it has hardly begun. (Video-on-demand in your home is a good example.)

In health care it is incredibly important to distinguish between the median and the edge. We have run into this trap many times. Forecasts that capitation would take over health care were rife in the early 1990s, even though less than 10 percent of doctors were in the group practices capable of absorbing capitation and the rest showed remarkably little interest in it. The problem wasn't just with the forecast but with the strategic behavior of decision makers such as hospital CEOs: They behaved as if capitation were the mainstream by buying doctors, integrating vertically, and all that good stuff. Similarly, we have prematurely extrapolated Medicare+Choice enrollment, physician practice management, and the electronic medical record (a permanently emerging technology).

Sometimes the edge becomes the median. For example, managed care in various forms virtually eliminated unfettered fee for service. Internet to the home has become the median, and the average American uses it as a source of health information, although not for e-health services and transactions, which remain an edge phenomenon.

So what do you do? First, be honest and clear in your language and in your thinking about the future. Try to distinguish between the median and the edge. Futurists and forecasters use terms such as *early adopters, wildcards,* and *harbingers* to talk about edge phenomena, and terms like *key driving forces, megatrends,* and *structural shifts* to describe changes in the median.

Second, develop good metrics of the emerging reality. I am a big believer that if something is going to be a big deal in the future, it's got to start sometime. That's why surveys are so useful in measuring the real progress toward a new future, a new median. I have had a partnership with pollsters Harris Interactive for more than twenty years because most forecasting is based on a good understanding of the present.

Third, learn to look for what Malcolm Gladwell calls *tipping points*—the points at which phenomena start to grow or decline exponentially. (Others have termed this *discontinuous change* or *inflection points.*) Surveys will help you measure the diffusion curve of new trends. Once you have a few data points, you can do the math.

But you have to have a nose for the emerging trends to even ask the right question in surveys. That's why the final tip is to keep a good ear to the ground. Conferences, networking with experts and peers, and reading good journals can alert you to candidates for the edge and give you a better sense of the mainstream.

Pearl Harbor, the Tipping Point, and Glacial Erosion

*Change happens for different reasons
and in different ways.*

I have been a student of structural change in society for thirty-five years. I started as an undergraduate at Edinburgh University, studying how the Scottish Highlands were transformed by a combination of political, economic, and cultural forces in the eighteenth century (not exactly the kind of scholarship that garners job offers). As a graduate student in urban planning, I studied how cities develop and change, and how they can be changed for the better through public and private investment and leadership. As a futurist and consultant, I have analyzed trends and developed scenarios, and tried to help my clients prepare for and respond to change. I've learned that you cannot predict the future, but that doesn't mean you can't think systematically about it.

Change happens in many ways, of course, and for many reasons, but in thinking about the prospects for structural change in health care (such as big health care reform, or a shift in paradigm toward prevention, or a rise of true consumer-directed health care), three simple models might help.

Pearl Harbor

The dreadful attack on Pearl Harbor on December 7, 1941, brought a reluctant United States into World War II and changed the course of world affairs. American blood and treasure helped liberate and reconstruct Europe and transformed Japan into a modern state, fundamentally altering the global economy.

At a global health care meeting, a senior British health official once remarked that health care in America would not fundamentally change without a "medical Pearl Harbor." He speculated that it would take avian flu, SARS (severe acute respiratory syndrome), or some event-driven crisis or disaster to completely transform the health care system. This has been a popular notion in health policy: that Americans respond best to crisis and that it will take an event-driven form of change to move the system in a meaningful way. (In hindsight, crisis was a key metaphor in bringing health care reform legislation to a head.)

The Tipping Point

Malcolm Gladwell changed our vocabulary forever with his excellent book *The Tipping Point*. In this form of change, circumstances, trends, and people conspire to create a tipping point where complex social systems go off in a different direction and change rapidly to a new state.

Again in health policy, tipping point theories and metaphors are always popular. Hey, I've used them myself. In one tipping point model of change, aging Baby Boomers, burdened by ever-escalating out-of-pocket costs and the looming financial chasm of retirement, reach a point where they tip toward asking for a bigger role for government funding and regulation.

Similar tipping points have been argued with regard to drug prices or even a backlash against overweight, unhealthy people by the well behaved and buff who refuse to pay the subsidy from well to sick that is implicit in all health insurance. (The concept of disruptive innovation, or discontinuous change brought about by technology, falls into this general tipping point category.)

Glacial Erosion

A third model of change is glacial erosion: huge forces that move slowly and inexorably with great power that can grind down mountains, scoop out valleys, and totally alter the landscape. I would argue that this is the most common form of change in American health care (okay, a wee bit quicker than glacial erosion, but play with me here). For example:

Demographic change. We get older one year at a time. It's a pretty slow process. The percentage of population over age sixty-five in the United States has moved from 11.2 percent in 1980 to 12.5 percent in 2000 (compared with 9 percent and 17 percent in Japan in the same period). When Baby Boomers start turning sixty-five in 2012, we will see a bigger jump—to 16.6 percent in 2020—but that is still a way off. In addition, all the respected academic literature shows that aging per se has a very small impact on the growth in utilization (a 1 percent to 2 percent per annum increase) that doesn't nearly explain double-digit cost increases.

Cost shifting. While it is true that cost shifting to consumers might wake them up and cause them to go to the barricades to demand major health care reform, we saw little evidence of this in the polls up until 2006. The reason may be that these changes are incremental, diffused, insidious, and experienced very differently depending on your circumstances. It took a lot of coverage erosion before the ice dam broke and coverage expansion was enacted.

The rising costs of high-tech care. One core driver of expense is our unwillingness to control, harness, regulate, or suppress the use or profitability of new medical technology. Americans like the idea of technology and innovation. Many of our leading economists tell us we are getting good value from this innovation in terms of life extension and quality of life (even though Koreans spend less than 20 percent per capita on health care and live longer) and we seem incapable individually or collectively of saying no to high-tech interventions whether they are cost-effective or not. I do not anticipate that we will suddenly get tough on technology anytime soon. We may ask for discounts, or even some price controls, but in general, we want the new stuff. Save for the funding of comparative effectiveness research in the stimulus bill, we have no institutions to limit the spread of marginally effective but expensive technologies.

Health care as a superior good. The international comparative health care data tell us that the richer a nation gets, the higher proportion of its GDP goes to health care. (This argument breaks down at the micro-economic level in the United States because of the regressive—premium rather than taxes—nature of our financing. Rich people pay a much smaller share of their income for health care as they get richer, but let's not let data interfere with the general point.) As costs rise and more costs are shifted to consumers, the top 10 percent of households based on income are probably going to be fine (meaning they can pay for both medicine and merlot). Even the top third of households may be okay. But the rest of us may be trading health care for cars, vacations, or even food.

Together, these long-term, glacially slow processes may accumulate and radically alter the landscape just as glaciers did in the physical world. If the glacial processes of change come to dominate the event-driven (Pearl Harbor) or tipping point models of change, here is what to expect:

- Huge and widening disparities in cost, quality, and service based on income of the patient
- Large and growing out-of-pocket costs for all, regardless of income and wealth
- Higher taxes for everybody (because on the one hand the ranks of Medicare and Medicaid must grow because of the glacial demographic forces we describe, and on the other hand because we are not heartless bastards, yet, and we will not leave people with absolutely nothing)
- Lower reimbursement and profit per unit (maybe, but you technology vendors enjoy the inverse trend for the moment)
- A perpetual sense of system in crisis (even after health care reform)

I have been anticipating structural change in America for twenty-five years. Eli Ginzberg, formerly of Columbia University, was a mentor and colleague to many of us students of structural change before he passed away, and he always counseled us to not over-anticipate massive structural change. As he said, the system may just "schlep along" forever. We will spend more, we will complain, and nothing will stop it. He was thinking glacial erosion, not tipping points or Pearl Harbor. And he was probably right.

If Bernie Madoff
Ran Health Care

*The Ponzi artist and our health care system
have more in common than we'd like to admit.*

We have had a lot of talk about reliable, sustainable reductions in health care costs. "Bend the trend" has become the new mantra. So I joked to a friend that we need someone like Bernie Madoff in health care to pull off the seemingly impossible: consistent performance that "bend the trend" requires.

Convinced that someone else probably had the same idea, I went to the mother of all plagiarism prevention tools (Google) to see if anyone had used the metaphor. Well, of course someone had. Christopher Hayes of *The Nation* wrote a great piece saying that listening to Rick Scott (the once disgraced and now resurrected ex-CEO of Columbia/HCA, recently turned Obama health care reform opponent and now Republican governor of Florida) was the equivalent of putting Bernie Madoff in charge of securities regulation. Funny.

But this essay is not about Rick Scott spending big money to discredit health reform and then run for governor. It addresses the more serious question (okay, not so serious): What if Bernie Madoff ran health care? What would health care look like?

Health care would grow every year, in good years and bad. Bernie Madoff was able to consistently grow in good years and bad. His investors got close to double-digit growth every single year for the last twenty years. Yet, health care has grown absolutely consistently since records began in the late 1920s at a rate about 2.5 percent above the GDP per capita. This makes Bernie look like a *putz*.

Clients would be very happy. People loved Bernie; they were very happy. Few complained about the service or the performance. My colleagues at Harris Interactive and the Harvard School of Public Health and I have been in partnership for over twenty years measuring public opinion and trying to make sense of it. Harris Interactive polls for 2009 show that 81 percent of Americans are very or somewhat satisfied with their ability to see a doctor whenever needed (compared with 79 percent in 1990), 81 percent are very or somewhat satisfied with their insurance benefits (up from 71 percent in 1990), and 58 percent are very or somewhat satisfied with their out-of-pocket costs for health care services (compared with 54 percent in 1990).

In addition, only 26 percent of Americans agree that "the health care system has so much wrong with it that we need to completely rebuild it," compared with 41 percent back in 1991 and down from its more recent peak of 37 percent in 2006. Bernie and health care were doing a good job, so why do we need all this change?

It would be hard to get in. "I know Bernie, I can get you in" was the mantra of the Upper East Side elite. You had to wait to get in. So, too, for health care. A Harris Interactive poll, conducted for the Commonwealth Fund in 2005 among sicker adults, showed that 23 percent of Americans waited six days or longer for a doctor appointment the last time they were sick or needed medical attention, compared with only 3 percent in New Zealand, 10 percent in Australia, 13 percent in Germany, and 15 percent in the United Kingdom. Only Canada, with 36 percent, had a worse performance than the United States. Bernie would appreciate the barriers to entry.

Make the European jet set think that Americans have the best system in the world. Bernie had all the rich and famous of Europe, the Middle East, and Russia convinced that he had the best system in the world. Bernie's better off in jail than being pursued by the Russian mob around Manhattan, but they used to look up to him. So, too, for health care. Fox News is full of experts, like expatriate Canadians, telling tales of rationing and restriction in every health care system but the good ole USA.

Make sure rich and influential people think you are good. Bernie had all the rich and influential people infatuated with his success. In health care, every hospital I know is at the 99th percentile of consumer satisfaction, and most of the 4,000-plus U.S. hospitals are in the top 100. Even though studies show there is no correlation among all the rating and ranking measures, we see a lot of affluent, well-insured Americans believing that their local hospital is superior, and rarely do they check if there are any data to support this.

Poor people would subsidize rich people. Bernie took money from poor people's pension funds to pay for reliable returns for the rich. Health care actually tends to subsidize the overconsumption of health insurance and health services by the rich at the expense of the poor and middle-income folks, because of the regressive way we pay for health care and the tax deductibility of health benefits.

The people on the nineteenth floor would never know what the people on the seventeenth floor were doing. Bernie never let even his closest associates go from the main office on the nineteenth floor of the Lipstick building to the seventeenth floor, where all the shenanigans were going on. No one got to see the real books.

In health care, the folks at Dartmouth (with a little help from Atul Gawande) have emerged as the intellectual foundation of health reform. It is well deserved: They are national treasures. Based on their analysis of the threefold variation in the utilization of services among Medicare recipients across the country, Dartmouth researchers estimate we could spend 30 percent less on health care for the same or even better outcomes. President Obama and Peter Orszag were all about the *Dartmouth Atlas* during the debate. But, even with all this great research, we don't know the full story because we are relying on lessons learned from Medicare data.

I constantly come across paradoxes in my travels. For example, why does a prominent hospital system in Northern California show up as so cost-effective based on Medicare data when so many of the health plans it deals with believe it is price gouging on commercial patients? Or why do the very-high-performance Medicare states, such as Wisconsin, have hospitals charging three times the Medicare rates to commercial insurers? Or why do studies that show all-payer inpatient data on cost and quality show little or no correlation between costs and quality either way, except for the finding that for-profit hospitals tend to be cheaper and worse? (Bring back Rick Scott?) Health care providers love to obfuscate, so we need to know the whole story. Let's do Dartmouth-style analysis with all the data and let the chips fall where they may.

There would be pay for referrals. Bernie would pay the feeder funds commission to bring him business. Atul Gawande's brilliant *New Yorker* article "The Cost Conundrum" exposed McAllen, Texas, where South Texas rancher-surgeons were screwing the federal government to boost the local economy by paying for referrals.

There would be self-dealing. Bernie kept it all close doing his own fake trades and dealing with his feeder-fund partners who were on the take. Self-referral is rife in American health care, fueled by frustrated doctors in search of new income streams in imaging, oncology drug administration, and routine testing.

Oversight and accountability would be brushed off as meddling. Bernie had his skeptics who went to the Securities and Exchange Commission and complained, but he brushed the critics and the regulators aside as meddlers in a marketplace that was benefiting people. Many in health care are resistant to more oversight, transparency, accountability, and public reporting. We avoid this at our collective peril.

Hide behind community benefit and philanthropy. Bernie was loved not just for his returns but for his good work. He was the doyen of the Jewish philanthropy circuit in New York and Palm Beach; he was adored for his compassion. Hospitals have done a good job of leading with their community benefit face. Although, I have to say, I still struggle with the notion that the gap between the chargemaster and what a payer actually negotiates is community benefit. I would relabel it as "the margin we would have gotten in a world of unlimited resources paid by people so stupid or rich that they didn't bother to negotiate." Doesn't sound so good, though.

Don't have really big accounting firms as auditors. Bernie used a solo guy in a strip mall to keep his books; no Big 4 here. Who does the books in health care? Are we sure we really know what's going on? Where were the auditors in McAllen, Texas? Where were the board finance committees? How many physician corporations get properly audited? I don't know, but given that U.S. health care is larger than the entire Chinese economy, there may be some interesting stuff going on.

Finally, you'd get found out, and it would leave your customers bankrupt. Bernie got caught. Many of his investors were wiped out. Innocent people were devastated, worthy philanthropies were annihilated, and lives were destroyed. In some ways, too, health care is being found out. It is certainly no Ponzi scheme, but it is unsustainable. It will bankrupt the country. It already is bankrupting individual households: 62 percent of bankruptcies were related to medical costs in 2007, according to Harvard researchers.

If something seems too good to be true, it probably is. We need to reform the health care system, and we may need to make some hard choices and some sacrifices. After all, we don't want to end up like Bernie and his clients.

On patient care

Compassion, Connection, and Concern

*I want my health care providers to understand
the emotions I'm feeling when I'm under their care.
It's likely I'm frightened, anxious, and in pain.*

I grew up in Britain, in the Basil Fawlty school of customer service—
customer as scum—which probably explains my low-level Maslowian view of most service businesses. I don't need to self-actualize at
my bank, I just need it to clear the checks I write (yet even this it
finds challenging).

All services should at least meet the basic Maslowian need of safety.
Safe schools, safe airlines, safe hospitals should be a goal. The bril-
liance of the patient safety movement was that it set up a discussion
of the lack of systems in health care by appealing to the most basic
of needs. Great service companies like Charles Schwab or Starbucks
have great systems (the information systems and the organizational
capacity) to deliver consistent quality.

Beyond safety, most of us look for competence. Is the technical
quality there? That's harder to judge in health care—how do we
know if our doctor does it right? Despite all the scorecards, most
of us judge on subjective factors. Many patients in surveys claim to
have changed doctors because they were dissatisfied with quality.
It probably was not based on systematic analysis of the technical
quality of the care, more that the physician didn't connect with the
patient, didn't spend enough time with him, didn't seem to care.

Comfort and convenience matter. The physical environment of health care is often intimidating, and caregivers are so harried they often don't have time to make the patient feel comfortable. But why do we agonize over the nursing shortage and not over a bank teller shortage? Because banking has redesigned itself, with ATMs, to serve customers more efficiently. We have not redesigned health care delivery to maximize quality, customer service, and caring.

Caring is the key part of the health care experience. I am not talking about an affable bedside manner. I don't want an excessively cheerful surgeon, kneeling by my bedside saying "Hi, I'm Bob. I'll be your surgeon today." God forbid that we turn the bedside into the same insincere, way-too-perky customer service we get in chain steakhouses.

I want caregivers who recognize that I am vulnerable. No matter how smart, well informed, and empowered I may be as patient, friend, or family member, when I come in contact with the health care system I am frightened, anxious, and in pain.

Health care systems need to transform health care delivery to match the best in breed of the service industry in safety, competency, and consistency of customer service. But as we embark on the grand redesign of health care over the next twenty years, let us not neglect the caring part of the health care experience. We need to reduce medical errors, but we also need compassion, connection, and concern.

Being on *60 Minutes*

Negative media coverage
can destroy a hospital's reputation.

You don't want to be on *60 Minutes*. Bottom line, unless you are the hot new celebrity, technology, or world leader, being on *60 Minutes* is, generally speaking, a pretty good signal that you are in trouble as an institution, industry, or individual. In the 1990s, managed care was the prime target. I used to joke back then that if it wasn't for managed care, *60 Minutes* would be called *30 Minutes*. In the early 2000s it was the drug companies taking the heat, whether because of excess profits or concerns over safety of drugs like Vioxx and Celebrex. Being exposed on *60 Minutes* is the epitome of demonization.

But demonization is a complex process. In the words of my colleague Humphrey Taylor, chairman of the Harris Poll, "The media is a mirror, a magnifying glass, and a prism: It reflects, amplifies, and distorts public opinion." The Harris Poll has documented the plummeting fortunes of many industries that become demons in the eyes of the media and the public, particularly in health care. But demonization really matters, as I pointed out in my book *Healthcare in the New Millennium: Vision, Values, and Leadership* (Jossey-Bass, 2002), because it has a profound effect on both public policy and private strategy. In the 1990s, the managed care industry faced the threat of regulation and a potential enactment of a patient's bill of rights, in the public policy arena. Similarly, the public's reaction to restrictions on choice of specialists and second-guessing of medical decisions by managed care "bureaucrats" led directly to an open-network, consumer-directed world, where we can have any health care we want—as long as we pay for it out of pocket. We all miss the bad old days of managed care.

On the Hot Seat

It is quite possible we will live to regret the demonization of pharmaceuticals (brought about by their own pricing, safety performance, and marketing track records) if we end up whacking the industry through price controls. The industry's naive defense to date ("pay me or I will stop developing new medicines") has worn thin and has developed an almost Tony Soprano–like tone with the media and the public. Obviously, we could regulate the industry to be like a utility, as some such as Marcia Angell have argued, and we would still have drug companies doing research. But just how innovative is your local electric utility? My neighborhood still has poles and wires put up shortly after the Ohlone Indians and the Mexican ranchers left the Bay Area.

Better for the pharmaceutical industry to heal itself, lower its prices, and change its business model to be better, faster, cheaper, and safer—not more expensive and worse. We need innovation, and we should be willing to pay for it, but it has to be noticeable improvement, not just statistically significant improvement.

Before the hospitals and doctors out there start gloating, let me suggest that you all are next. One of the reasons industries get demonized is that when consumers have to pay more they get very, very cranky. In a world of consumer payment and retail care, how do we feel about our doctors and hospitals when we are writing big checks with our own money? Doctors are still trusted and revered, so they have a lot of falling to do if the patients and the public turn on them. For hospitals, the demonization has already started. Class action lawsuits about price gouging of uninsured patients were just the beginning of greater public scrutiny and political pressure on the economics of well-to-do, nonprofit hospitals. Medical errors, fraud and abuse, and patient safety concerns have made *60 Minutes* already. All of this negative attention may lead to public policy aimed at whacking hospital reimbursement or redefining tax-exempt status, if the hospital sector does not try to manage the public mood.

Looking Like the Good Guy

What do you do about it?

First, prepare to be demonized when you make consumers pay more. You have to articulate value to the customer—before, during, and after the service is performed—and you have to be very smooth, efficient, warm, and fuzzy on the collections process. Does this sound like your collections process? Health care organizations of all types are absolutely horrible at bill presentment and payment systems. We have the explanation of benefits forms (EOBs), but they don't explain anything. Maybe the consumer-directed health care pioneers can actually teach us how to do this stuff properly.

Second, you have to build, constantly reinforce, and continuously measure reputation and trust. I have said it before in my essays: Hospitals that lose the trust of their local community are toast.

Finally, think about your behavior before you take action, whether it is a big strategic decision or a small step in a business process, and ask the question: How will this look on *60 Minutes*?

Pimp My Ride

*An MTV show in which beat-up cars
receive flashy makeovers is all too reminiscent
of our health care system.*

If you have teenage kids, you end up watching a lot of MTV; otherwise, you have nothing to talk to your children about. My kids have both graduated from college now, but they got me hooked. My favorite show of all time is *Pimp My Ride.* The show is in the genre of makeover reality television. In this case a rapper-host introduces a poor kid and his or her beaten-up old car (the ride). The car is taken from the young adult and transformed by a team from West Coast Custom (a body shop and customization company in Los Angeles).

Each episode shows a different kid and a different car: clapped-out Pintos; beaten-up Suburbans; and a plethora of ugly, weird, old, and dilapidated camper/truck hybrids. The process is always the same: They strip the car's interior and install an unbelievable array of stereo equipment (woofers and subwoofers included) and video displays (even laptops), and the whole thing is topped off with an amazing paint job in vibrant blue or dazzling yellow, with custom painted flames on the side. They never seem to do anything to the engine, drive train, or chassis of these vehicles. At the close of each episode the youngsters are shown the transformed vehicle that has been "pimped," and they can never contain their excitement. They are deeply grateful.

The prevailing vision of quality in the American health care system is *Pimp My Ride*.

We take a really bad chassis and engine (the health care system) and bolt unbelievable amounts of high technology onto this tired, old, and ineffective frame. We spend extravagantly on buildings, machines, drugs, devices, and people at West Coast Custom Health Care. The people who own the rides are very grateful because they don't have to pay for the service (high-deductible, catastrophic, PPO coverage is the norm in America; once enrollees have met their deductible and are ensconced in an American hospital, the sky's the limit). It all looks great, has a fantastic sound, and sports comfortable seats, but it will break down if you try to drive it anywhere.

Pimp My Ride is a perfect metaphor for the health care system as a whole, but it also applies to the individual patient. We take the morbidly obese, the terminally ill, and the very old and throw fabulous technology and unbelievable paint jobs at them. (Apparently, a young resident at Harvard made the observation on National Public Radio about treating the terminally ill that it was like *Pimp My Ride*. I am not above stealing ideas from my friends at Harvard, but in this case it was great minds thinking alike.)

From the system as a whole to the treatment of individual patients, we need to break the *Pimp My Ride* mentality. First, we need to transform the basic engine and drive train. We need a new system of medical care delivery and the reimbursement to support it.

Second, we need to examine the level of technology, facilities, services, and intensity of care that yields the optimal outcome. We keep throwing money and technology at problems without asking basic questions, such as: What should be done, how much, for whom, when?

Third, we need some intelligent consumer engagement. The kid who gets his beater fixed by MTV could care less how much it costs, just as we patients could care less about the cost of excessive esoterica we receive in the hospital. While I have been a critic of dumb-cost shifting and simplistic high-deductible health plans, I do believe we have to engage the consumer intelligently in understanding and participating in the financial consequences of high-technology interventions that are marginally effective.

Finally, we have to break the public perception that the medical equivalent of a good paint job and a fancy sound system makes for good quality. The Institute of Medicine and its followers have a long way to go because the prevailing vision of quality health care among most doctors and most patients is closer to *Pimp My Ride* than to the Institute of Medicine's noble vision.

Simple Care

*Don't let complexity be an excuse
for inadequate care.*

American health care is large and complex—larger, indeed, than
the entire Italian economy and about as well organized. Recent
advances have made it more complex—medically, organizationally,
and administratively. For example, genomic medicine will increasingly require that care be customized to a patient's individual
genetic profile. While this is not yet in the mainstream, the trend
is clear. Similarly, benefit carve-outs, specialty disease management
organizations, and focused factories including specialty hospitals
and clinics all fuel the organizational complexity of the system.
In addition, changes in reimbursement and benefit design—from
the Byzantine complexity of Medicare Part D arrangements to
pay-for-performance, tiered networks, and consumer cost-sharing
arrangements—make the health care system more impenetrable for
patient and provider alike.

The many regulatory provisions of Obamacare, both those already
defined and those to come, will make the health care system even
more complicated. While this complexity is a natural outgrowth of
the heterogeneity of a big country, a manifestation of American pluralism, and a legacy of incrementalism in policy, we sometimes hide
behind the complexity and use it as an excuse for not doing the right
thing.

The Canadian Viewpoint

My wife, Nora, is Canadian. Like most Canadians, she is pretty mystified by the complexity of the American health care system. She is a seasoned emergency room nurse; she is also a no-nonsense prairie girl from Manitoba (it's like Minnesota, only colder). But while she has the Midwestern nice, she also takes no prisoners.

She grew up in a medical family and worked in critical care in Canada and the United States. She was a nursing systems analyst and manager, doing clinical reengineering before it became fashionable. I respect and draw on her experience and perspective on all things, especially health care. To listen to Nora, it's easy to fix the American health care system.

Nora's major beef is complexity. Why does it all have to be so complex? In her view, health care is simple:

Develop a standard of care. There should be a standard of care for every procedure—from prevention, through primary care, to complex operations. The standard of care should be developed by professionals based on the best available scientific evidence. Providers should follow the standard of care and should be sanctioned through professional peer review if they don't.

Use a set fee schedule. There should be a standard fee schedule for all patients and all providers, and there should be a standard claim form that everyone uses. (An estimated 25 percent of American health care is administrative waste motion in which armies of clerks battle over payment.) When pushed on the issue of whether all providers should get the same payment, Nora concedes that there should be a basic standard for all providers, but if providers deliver superior performance, then they should be rewarded not just through volume but also through price. Still, her basic question is: "Why aren't all providers achieving the high level of performance of the best cohort, if they are following the standard of care, eh?"

Provide transparency. Nora knows that it is politically impossible to have a single-payer system in the United States. Americans are not Canadian. She even concedes that there is some benefit to having the consumer pay something toward his or her care at the point of service. This is a view shared by most Canadian providers, by the way, who live daily with the consequences of unrestrained access to primary care. But what Nora has a great deal of difficulty with is that there is no price list in American health care. We Morrisons are a well family, but Nora spends hours on the phone hassling with Stanford, WellPoint, Aetna, and United trying to get a clear explanation of what things cost, what was covered, what we owe, and why. It is not an explanation of benefits (EOB); it is an obfuscation of benefits (OOB). While Nora is an empowered consumer, she cannot get anyone in health care to tell her what something is going to cost in advance of having the service. How else are we supposed to decide?

Simplifying

What are the benefits of simplicity? Lower administrative costs, much greater consumer engagement, and less anguish among providers. But how should we proceed in such a complex system that is becoming progressively more complicated? Here are some examples:

Standardize care. The anesthesiologists have done a brilliant job of standardizing and enforcing clinical processes. The result has been improved patient safety, better outcomes, and lower malpractice costs.

Use flat co-insurance. A 20 percent co-insurance applied to all services up to an out-of-pocket maximum would make prices transparent to consumers and be a lot easier to understand than tiered formularies; tiered networks; and the arcane combination of co-payments, deductibles, and other cost-sharing arrangements. Even in the drug area we have resisted adopting co-insurance because pharmacists and pharmacy benefit management companies make more money on generics with a co-payment than with co-insurance (a $10 co-payment for a generic drug is better for them than co-insurance's 20 percent of $20). Hospitals and physicians won't look so good in a flat co-insurance world, and drugs (particularly generics) start looking like an even better deal.

Standardize enrollment processes. The California Healthcare Foundation's (CHCF) pioneering Health-e-App and One-e-App are standardized, electronic tools for enrolling eligible beneficiaries in public programs such as Medi-Cal and Healthy Families. As proud members of CHCF's board, my colleagues and I point to this as one of the foundation's key innovative contributions, even though the public programs may not always have the resources to accept the eligible enrollees. Indeed, CHCF's chief program officer, Sam Karp, was asked to co-chair a White House task force on administrative simplification for enrollment under health reform.

Standardize benefit designs. Health insurers are creating myriad choices for the customer—too much choice. The ridicule that Medicare Part D arrangements have earned from cartoonists and *Saturday Night Live* is because of the mind-boggling complexity of the choices. When I signed on to the www.Medicare.gov Web site, the first thing it told me was to download a Flash Media Player. I had visions of grannies across America having to take a course in installing Java applets.

It is quite likely that the future modifications to Medicare Part D will involve simplifying and regulating the number of choices available to consumers. Similarly, as health reform regulations emerge, we may see more emphasis on administrative simplification. But it should not stop there. Simple, standardized care and administrative processes can lead to better consumer engagement, lower costs, elimination of variation and disparities, and better quality. Isn't that what we want? Let's not hide our inefficiency behind a veil of complexity.

With Mayo

In the deli that is health care,
we all deserve the special.

In the fall of 2006, I was with Mayo. Not in the sandwich sense, but in the Rochester, Minnesota, folks at the Mayo Clinic sense. It was my second visit, this time to meet with the leaders of Mayo Health System.

Mayo Health System is not the Rochester clinic but the network of sixteen affiliated hospitals and clinics with 720 physicians spread over 250 miles where Minnesota, Wisconsin, and Iowa meet. Mayo Health System is part of the consolidated financials of the Mayo Clinic (which in total has some $6 billion in revenue from all its sites). But from a governance perspective, Mayo Health System reports to the board of trustees of the Mayo Clinic Rochester. Got it?

Once-independent community hospitals and clinics have been absorbed into this network over the last fourteen years. The progressive integration that has occurred under the able leadership of Dr. Peter Carryer, chair of the Mayo Health System board, and his colleagues has created a network that gets progressively more Mayo over time, exhibiting ever more characteristics of the mission, values, and behavior of the mother ship in Rochester. Actually, *mother ship* is the wrong term, more like mother fleet, because the whole of Rochester, with the exception of the giant Libby's corn-on-the-cob water tower, seems to be part of the Mayo Clinic—from the myriad hospitals and clinic buildings to the fact that everyone on the regional jets flying into Rochester is going to the clinic to get treatment, to get training, or to give a talk.

I came away, once again, from Mayo even more firmly of the belief that we all deserve to have the Mayo Clinic: not to all fly to Rochester, please understand—there isn't room on the planes or in the Marriott next door—but to have our local health system deliver the Mayo.

Lessons from Mayo

What makes Mayo? My friend Len Berry, PhD, distinguished business professor at Texas A&M and an internationally recognized expert in service industries, spent a lengthy sabbatical studying Mayo in Scottsdale, Arizona, and Rochester, and I cannot even begin to do justice to his scholarly review of what makes Mayo so good. (You should read it for yourself. See, for example, "Clueing in Customers," by Leonard L. Berry and Neeli Bendapudi, *Harvard Business Review*, 2003, reprint R0302H.) But here are a few personal observations I would add to Len's work about what factors distinguish Mayo from the pack.

Global brand. The Mayo Clinic is synonymous with quality. No, really, it is. It has a global brand that speaks of medical excellence in solving difficult diagnostic problems, of providing desperately sick patients with hope and offering path-breaking medical advances in research and treatment. That's why patients come from all over the world to get care and why Mayo has more than 1,700 clinical fellows receiving training in graduate medical education. "I trained at Mayo" is a proud boast of many of the world's greatest clinicians and medical scientists.

Saudi princes and a lot of locals. Despite Mayo's globally recognized brand, it is important to know that only 3.5 percent of patients come from afar. I am sure these patients represent a bigger share of the bottom line, maybe 10 to 15 percent, but it always comes as a bit of a surprise to find that Mayo is a regional and local health system at its core. Mayo remains financially healthy because the local Blues plans pay a fairly high share of reasonable and customary charges. If these plans started to get difficult, Mayo might have a problem, but I can't imagine why a payer would take them on; what's not to like about getting the right care the first time around?

So, even at Mayo, health care is primarily a local good. Actually, this local-versus-national focus isn't that much different from any of the national flagships like the Cleveland Clinic, M.D. Anderson, Stanford, Hopkins, Cedars-Sinai, Mass General, and on and on. While these great institutions attract patients from all over the world and these (generally affluent) patients contribute a disproportionate share of the bottom line, they tend to account for less than 5 percent of volume. Funnily enough, just the other day, I landed in Cleveland and as we pulled into the gate, across the way was an Airbus emblazoned with the government of Kuwait colors. At first, I was shocked that there was a direct flight from Kuwait to Cleveland, and then I realized it was probably some ailing emir who commandeered the government jet to come and get a bypass at the Cleveland Clinic.

Values-based culture. In the early days of Mayo, one of the clinic's founders, William J. Mayo, MD, stated: "The best interest of the patient is the only interest to be considered." Mayo is built on this simple premise that the founding Mayo brothers hammered into the DNA of the organization: "Put the patient first." This is not a slogan. It is the credo that guides the organization and the people who work there. Len Berry's research reveals a staff at Mayo Clinic highly committed to serving patients. From volunteers to world-class surgeons to the more than 70,000 individual benefactors, the people at Mayo are focused on the best interests of the patient.

Minnesota nice meets medical excellence. As Berry and Bendapudi's research shows, Mayo carefully captures this will to serve and reinforces it through training, selection of staff, and a structure of compensation (salaried physicians in particular) that rewards integration and teamwork to serve patients' needs. It doesn't hurt that Mayo is in the "nice" state of Minnesota, but these values and practices apparently extend to the Scottsdale and Jacksonville, Florida, campuses as well.

No jerks. In my limited exposure to Mayo, I would argue that one of the hallmarks is that it doesn't hire jerks. This is not a place for brilliant but difficult prima donnas. The folks at Mayo say they may have the odd jerk, but he or she is the exception rather than the rule. When physicians and staff are recruited, they get the no-jerks-allowed message, so the people who are attracted to Mayo tend to be self-selected to this culture of getting along to serve patients.

Team is everything. Integrated, team-based care is the hallmark of the Mayo delivery model. If your doctor can't figure out the problem, he or she will bring in colleagues to help, and there is no shame in drawing on others' expertise. While this is how medicine is supposed to work, it doesn't always turn out that way in many large, internally competitive, clinical settings that operate more like *Survivor.*

No empire building. Unlike many big, prestigious academic medical centers, there is remarkably little sense of departmental empire building at Mayo. Partly this is reinforced by the fact that important physician leadership roles (such as chairman of the board of trustees of the Mayo Clinic at Rochester) are for four-year terms, and while in some cases an exceptional incumbent may serve two terms, it is anticipated that they will return to full-time clinical practice or some other combination of duties after their leadership service concludes. (In the interests of full disclosure, my wife's first cousin, Dr. Hugh C. Smith, a distinguished cardiologist, recently concluded two such terms as Rochester Clinic board chair and has now returned to a combination of clinical practice and development work on behalf of the clinic. So if my essay seems uncharacteristically positive, you skeptics might attribute it to family-oriented bias.)

No expansion beyond two satellites. While Mayo has successful satellites in Arizona and Florida, it seems the organization has settled on the formula that it doesn't have to be everywhere in America to serve patients. Indeed, by focusing locally it can sustain and enhance the model without having the values and vision corrupted by the pressures of competition in a whole bunch of different geographic markets with very different medical mind-sets.

Leading health and health care. Mayo has been a pioneer in public education on health and wellness; it plays a key role in health promotion nationally; and it is no accident that Olmsted County, where Rochester is located, is among the healthiest in the nation. Thankfully, the Mayo Clinic is also committed to becoming more of a voice in the national health policy debate, as evidenced by the Mayo Clinic CEO, Dr. Denny Cortes (now retired), who played a prominent role in the health reform debate.

We all deserve the Mayo Clinic. We all need truly integrated care, where the patient is put first; where the care is done right the first time; where the payer pays for value and outcomes, not low-cost units of service; and where staff are proud and happy to work, on behalf of patients. If that doesn't sound like the frenetic zoo where you work, or where you get health care, then maybe you should get your care with Mayo.

Ohio

Innovations in the heartland
are worth a closer look.

Most policy wonks, consultants, CEOs, and venture capitalists live a bicoastal existence, jetting between San Francisco, New York, Boston, and Washington, DC, and occasionally touching down at O'Hare in Chicago. They fly over the rest of *Amurrica*, often believing, mistakenly, that nothing new or interesting happens there.

Regarding health care, they are wrong. Many of the more innovative health care organizations, including regional coalitions, health plans, hospitals, and health systems, can be found in the middle of America. I have had the opportunity to work with many of those organizations over the years, but I would draw attention to Ohio as a good example of quiet innovation where institutions are making a difference without all the fanfare and self-promotion of California and Massachusetts.

Midwest Successes

Ohio is the nation's seventh most populous state, with more than 11 million residents, and has proven to be a critical swing state in national elections. It's a state with several significant cities, including Cleveland, Columbus, Cincinnati, Dayton, Toledo, and the Akron/Canton metropolitan area (if people share an airport name, I figure they don't mind being lumped together). I have had an opportunity to visit several institutions in the state and have been impressed at many innovations and health care successes.

Cleveland. If you are going to have a heart attack, have it on the doorstep of the Cleveland Clinic. Under the leadership of pioneering heart surgeon Dr. Toby Cosgrove, the Cleveland Clinic continues to earn its reputation as a global leader in high-quality care and as a key generator of medical innovation. Much less heralded, though equally impressive, is the story of University Hospitals Health System (UHHS) in Cleveland, which has undergone a massive financial turnaround in the last four or five years under CEO Tom Zenty's leadership. UHHS successfully pursued Vision 2010, investing over a billion dollars in new development, while raising quality and reducing costs.

Dayton. At the nationally recognized Kettering Health Network, CEO Frank Perez is leading the system in rapidly implementing personal health records, not just for his own hospitals' patients but for the community at large. This ambitious, patient-centric initiative helps patients manage their own health and provide information to local physicians, improving the timeliness and quality of patient care.

Canton. Aultman Health System, providing nationally ranked quality in its facilities, has a long history of delivering high quality at low cost. Since 1985, Aultman has built its own health plan, AultCare, which serves 500,000 members in the local area (mostly through PPO products). Aultman Hospital doesn't need any other managed care contracts, as its value proposition to local employers is that it can deliver care better and more cheaply by taking the insurance dollar out of the community. This is a rare and high-performance example of virtual integration. CEO Ed Roth quietly builds on the Aultman legacy to provide the value proposition for the Canton community.

Cincinnati. The Greater Cincinnati Health Council celebrated its fiftieth anniversary recently. The council has been a pioneer in many areas of regional cooperation among hospitals and other stakeholders. Its pioneering work under current CEO Colleen O'Toole and her predecessor Lynn Olman has included path-breaking innovation in transparency of cost and quality measurement and reporting, in quality improvement, and in regional health information networks. These and other initiatives have won accolades and awards from The Joint Commission and the Robert Wood Johnson Foundation.

The council spawned a long-standing regional health information organization (RHIO), HealthBridge, which remains one of the few successful and self-sustaining RHIO business models in the country and is a tremendous platform for communitywide health management and disease management initiatives. Somehow HealthBridge has overcome the difficulties of infrastructure, privacy, complexity, standards setting, and lack of organizational commitment that have dogged so many of the RHIO efforts nationally.

Dublin. Ohio Health built a brand-new hospital, Dublin Methodist, to serve the expanding local community in the Columbus suburbs. CEO Cheryl Herbert and her team have created a new, evidence-based-designed facility that promises to be one of the highest state-of-the-art health care facilities in the country. Dublin Methodist is a living laboratory of how organizational culture and design can be melded to deliver a superior health care experience.

Three Lessons from Ohio

I am sure if I looked, I would find similar good work in other parts of the state. So to any Ohioans I've left out, please don't take offense. But my general point is this: While Ohio is not at the top of the pile in being one of the high-quality/low-utilization states, like Oregon and Minnesota, it has significant innovations in finance and delivery that are worthy of attention. I would make three observations about those innovations:

Leadership matters. In all cases, the institutions I ran into were blessed with good leaders—in many cases, two and three generations of such leaders. Leaders make a difference; it's not just a bumper sticker.

Local is good. Sometimes it's easier to get people around a table to act locally than to make plans and policy globally. This is not always the case: "All politics is local," they say, and my observation is that the more local it gets, the more vicious it gets. But somehow these local leaders have found a way to bring stakeholders together.

Look everywhere. The nation's business and policy elites need to stop flying over the middle of America and actually touch down, watch and listen to what is going on. You all might learn something.

On benefits
and spending

Wary of Choices

*Consumer responsibility may force
some improvements in health care,
but the less sophisticated users will be left behind.*

The health care consumer needs to have skin in the game is a phrase you hear frequently in health care. For those of you who don't play poker, it means we consumers ought to pay at the point of care, which will motivate us to make more informed, value-conscious choices. Every health plan CEO I know, and almost all large employers, see this as the big theme for health care. Consumer responsibility for payment will be sold to us consumers bundled with choice and couched in terms of empowerment. (Remember, when you hear the word *empowerment*, it's code for "You're on your own, pal!")

At the same time, we have increasing variation in health care. A recent Institute of Medicine report calls attention to the huge disparities in care based on race and socioeconomic status. Dartmouth College research over the last thirty years has pointed to great variation in medical care across the country and across very small geographic areas. The patient safety and quality measurement gurus tell us that there are enormous differences in the quality of care between institutions and within institutions. Efforts to standardize care have been thwarted by a lack of enthusiasm among providers. Indeed, practice guidelines and evidence-based medicine are viewed by most doctors as one step away from communism.

How will the newly empowered, value-conscious consumers make out in this highly variable world?

If I go to that happy place inside (or listen to my most optimistic colleagues at the purchasing coalitions and health care foundations across the country), I can imagine the value-motivated consumer forcing a recalcitrant provider community to work on the big problems of clinical redesign and process improvement. We consumers, armed with new performance data at the provider level, will have the information and incentives to kick clinical butt and make choices that keep providers on their toes and take the American health care system to a new level of quality and accountability. But when I allow my natural Scottish cynicism to rise, I hear myself saying: "Most costs are incurred by the sick or the unconscious. They are not in a good position to kick anyone's butt, let alone their doctor's. And we Americans already have more skin in the game than anyone else in the developed world, with little measurable improvement in the value of health care we receive."

Both of my inner voices are correct in their own way. Fine-grain performance metrics in the hands of motivated consumers will have positive effects on the way care is organized and delivered. Providers should not resist such metrics, but embrace them. At the same time, the most disadvantaged among us—the poor, the elderly, the uninsured (or underinsured) with chronic illnesses, or just those of us who are medically illiterate—will struggle mightily because they haven't the resources, knowledge, or support to navigate this new world.

The Old Course
and the MRI

*Only in America would doctors
recommend surgery to improve a golf score.*

In 2001, I had a serious problem requiring a medical intervention: My golf game had collapsed. For a Scot, this is the end of healthy living. I had injured my neck while lifting luggage, and believing that one ought to be conservative in treatment, I had undergone physiotherapy and traction (what medieval torturers called the rack). It produced only modest improvement in the symptoms (tingling in the fingers, weakness in the legs, and a constant neck tick resembling Tourette's) and the golf game.

My wife (a former critical care nurse) finally prodded me to return to my primary care physician. He suggested that I have an MRI. What a thrill for a Scottish-Canadian to have an MRI! It is easier for Canadians to win an Olympic Gold medal in figure skating than it is to get an MRI. No one in Canada has ever had one.

The MRI showed a significant herniated disk in my neck and some spinal cord damage. My neurosurgeon explained what he could do. This is not what he said, but it is what I heard: "First, we cut your throat, push the throat stuff aside, we go in, take out the disk, replace it with a piece of bone from dead Uncle Frank, and screw it all back together with a titanium plate."

My care at Stanford was fantastic: in on Monday, out on Tuesday, very little pain, and a very professional and caring staff. Although I did detect enormous opportunities for error, what with the constant handing over from one nursing team to another and the myriad people who came to see me, and lots of to-ing and fro-ing and form filling in various places in the hospital. I characterized my experience as "islands of clinical excellence surrounded by the Department of Motor Vehicles."

Over a year has passed, and the golf game is on the mend. On a visit to Scotland last summer, I played the Old Course at St. Andrews in a 40-mile-an-hour wind. I made an eagle on the par 5, 14th hole thanks to the following gale and a brilliant read on a 50-yard putt from my caddie. I was back, courtesy of American health care.

At a recent family wedding in Canada I asked Scottish doctor friends what would have happened to me if I were still back in Scotland. They said that the surgery was done in cases with serious clinical indications, adding that shooting a 100 was not classified as a disability in Britain. Indeed, Dr. Calum said: "Och, they would have told you to play from the white tees and putt better!"

I am deeply grateful to my doctors, to Stanford, and to my health insurers for restoring my ability to enjoy an important part of my life. My story is a metaphor: U.S. health care distinguishes itself from other systems by delivering such quality-of-life improvement, albeit at significant cost. Moreover, the quality of life can be improved only if you are well insured and can come up with the diagnostic down payment. But should the health care system pay for it all? Are there more deserving uses of the scarce resources? And who decides all this? What Americans want is a decent floor for all Americans and the right to trade up with their own money. We need to figure out how to bring this about. No one should have to give up golf.

Price Transparency
and the American Hospital

Let's see a price list for hospital procedures—
then we can decide if we really want lobster soup.

Almost twenty years ago, in a presentation to Tommy Frist (of HCA fame), a colleague and I showed a Conference Board survey in which hospitals were listed forty-ninth out of fifty items ranked on their value. Chicken was seen as the best value in America. Lawyers' fees were ranked forty-eighth.

Mr. Frist became upset, not because hospitals were near last, but because they were behind lawyers. We pointed out that the reason hospitals are seen as such a bad value is that they persist in sending the patient a bill after the care has been received. Who could justify $58 for Tylenol or hundreds of dollars for simple lab tests? Some wag in Mr. Frist's executive team said, "Yeah, in the future we shouldn't send the patient a bill. We should send them a chicken."

Fast-forward to 2004. The hospital reimbursement trends are now leading us toward consumer responsibility for payment, tiered networks, and transparency in pricing. We are going back to a health system in which consumers are exposed to a larger share of the cost of each of the health care silos. While these developments are subtly disguised as "consumer-directed health care" or "tiered networks," consumers will see how much the cost of a stay in a hospital will affect them in the pocketbook. Well, that's the theory.

On a wonderful, special trip to France last September, my wife and I splurged on an extravagant dinner in a fancy French hostelry in St. Emilion. As we were seated at the table, the maitre d' furnished me with a menu with prices on it and my wife (presumed to be less economically discriminating) with a menu that showed no prices. My wife offered that she might start with the lobster soup. I casually flashed the menu with the prices. ("Not for $43 a bowl," I suggested). After she enjoyed the green salad instead, we reflected on what this could mean for health care.

There is no price list in the American hospital. We patients are like guests at an expensive banquet, with no clue of what the lobster soup really costs. We select things (on those rare occasions in a hospital when we have such choices) completely oblivious to the cost to the patient or the third party paying the majority of the bill.

Thus, it is argued, consumers need to pay at the point of care and to be more frugal. Okay, then, show me the prices in advance, when I am conscious, upright, rational, and informed. How hard could this be? Car repair is as complicated as hernia repair, yet most Shell stations can give you a pretty decent estimate in advance—and they call you before spending more if they find something else wrong. (Is it just me, or do you always need two new tires when you take your car in?)

But hospital accounting is arcane and glacial at best, few hospitals know the true cost of clinical interventions, and fewer yet have the information systems to communicate such data in real time to a fully informed patient on the edge of clinical expenditure.

A lot of this patient responsibility for payment is silly. But if we are going down this road, please give us a menu with prices on it. And we will all live with the consequences: more green salad and chicken, and less lobster soup.

Dogs and Doctors

*We rely on physicians to choose our medicine
the way canines depend on us to buy their food.*

I've often joked that there is a unique field of health economics because of the special nature of health care, while there is no field of dog food economics. I suddenly realized that I am wrong. There is a remarkable similarity between health care economics and dog food economics. I had this epiphany while listening to a panel of health care experts debate the consumer's role in health care versus the role of managed care.

To economists, health care is different from other markets. The reason, they argue, is that there is asymmetry of information: Providers know what they are selling, while consumers largely do not know what they are buying. The asymmetry of information is the cause of market failure in health care and the reason the doctor plays such a special role as agent for the patient in the health care transaction. Third-party payment makes the issues even more complex, yet we buy other forms of insurance in a marketplace without the need for special agents.

Then it struck me. Dogs don't buy dog food. They may eat it, but they don't buy it. Dogs have preferences and may refuse to eat something (voting with their paws, so to speak), but they don't generally select the food they eat. Sometimes they have choice. My large and aged golden retriever has demonstrated that he prefers pepperoni pizza, prawns, and whole sticks of butter (given the opportunity to steal food) over the dry, boring pellets for overweight old dogs we feed him. Dogs rely on an agent (the owner) to help them make decisions and pay the tab.

In the past, we patients were just like the dogs. We knew what we didn't like, but all we could do was bitch about it (pardon the pun) and change doctors. Armed with information, we patients now are supposed to be intelligent consumers. Yet, I think to a large extent we do need to have some help. Harris Interactive surveys show that the square-root-of-zero humans (actually less than 1 percent) have ever made a decision on selecting a plan or doctor based on a report card they saw or read. Don't get me wrong—I am a big fan of report cards, and dog shows for that matter. But dog shows and report cards are more important to dog owners and providers than they are to dogs and patients.

Dogs need help, and patients do, too. There is still an important role for agency in health care. Clearly, we are moving away from the paternalistic notion that only the dog owner, or doctor, or health plan knows best. Managed competition put the consumer more in the decision-making role, but the plan sponsor helped orchestrate the choice of health plans and set the consequences for lack of cost-conscious choice. We do this with our dog, too: If he is foolish enough to steal pizza, he sleeps outside.

But the current trend toward consumer-directed health care doesn't give us much in the way of help. Health plans and purchasing coalitions are arming us with Web sites. Some sophisticated providers offer medical concierge services to help us navigate the complexity of health care. Yet, surveys show that we still rely heavily on our doctors and our friends and family to navigate the health care system. We trust them to do what's right, just like my dog trusts me.

Before we all get too carried away with consumerizing health care, we need to think through this issue of agency. As more responsibility for cost and choice is forced on the patient, it becomes both difficult and dangerous to ask the doctor to be both retailer to and trusted confidante of the patient. That's like asking her to be a cross between St. Thomas Aquinas and H&R Block: She has to do your tax return before she can prescribe anything. We need to develop a new cadre of trusted agents; otherwise health care will go to the dogs.

Tiers, Transparency, and Transformation

Tiered networks can shake up the game in a good way if we design them right.

We know there are enormous variations in medical care across the United States and even within small geographic areas. Dr. Jack Wennberg and his colleagues at Dartmouth have painstakingly documented these variations over the last thirty or more years. Most of the variations can be explained by two factors: (1) larger supply of providers (facilities and specialists) driving overall higher utilization and (2) provider preferences in use of diagnostic tests and procedures, where doctors simply do more for a given patient with a specific condition. These two factors combined can result in three- to fourfold variation in utilization and costs without any apparent differences in quality and outcome.

Fresh off the boat as an immigrant in Canada, I got my first health care job as an analyst for a consulting group that served the Vancouver teaching hospitals. One of my first projects (which turned into a seven-year gig as a researcher) was focused on clinical laboratory utilization. My boss was a pathologist interested in a few simple questions: Why do doctors order lab tests, and do they really need them? In a global budgeted world, these were prudent questions. We found a threefold variation in use of lab tests across a whole range of diagnoses (DRGs before they existed).

We presented our data to the clinical chiefs of Vancouver General Hospital: "Ya, but did you adjust for severity?" No, like dolts we hadn't. Off we went, hat in hand, and spent six months developing a case-mix adjustment index. Same answer: a threefold variation and a 5 percent to 10 percent per annum escalation in lab use for the same diagnosis. I have called this the "Ya, but" defense ever since: When doctors are challenged about their patterns of utilization, they always balk.

From Variation to Tiers

Fast-forward to today's threefold variation in use and costs that is not tied to quality. Tiered networks of hospitals, specialists, primary care, reference laboratories—you name it—are all becoming the rage. From Aetna to WellPoint, health plans are defining skinny networks where as few as 25 percent of the providers in a particular area are included. The goal of the proponents is to drive patients to these efficient, high-value providers through incentives. However, most doctors and hospitals are busy enough; they may be short of payment, but they aren't short of patients. If the high-value providers don't have the capacity to absorb more patients, at least the poor performers might be embarrassed into shaping up and emulating the high-performance folk in their clinical behavior. That's the theory.

But, like my colleagues in Vancouver twenty-five years ago, the delivery system will not go quietly. Hospitals and doctors who get placed in an economically disadvantaged tier (where the patient has to pay significantly more out of pocket for care) will bitch and complain. If the tiering is not based on transparent, scientific evidence, the provider system has a legitimate beef. This was the case in St. Louis, where United Healthcare hastily constructed a narrow network for General Motors employees that omitted a large proportion of specialists and hospitals, including the large, prestigious, and enormously ecumenical Barnes Christian Jewish Health System. Specialists in St. Louis went nuts.

In this case, United screwed up. It doesn't normally do that; it is usually pretty smart. But under pressure from a desperate GM—which had no other health care options, given the generosity of the United Auto Workers union contract and the prohibition on cost sharing—network design was the only choice GM had, and United listened to the customer. (Advice: Don't listen to your customers if they ask you to do something stupid.)

From Tiers to Transformation

Tiered networks can shake up the game in a positive way. But we must be very careful that the tiers are based on evidence, that the evidence is transparent, and that it passes the laugh test. You can't exclude the provider that everyone agrees is the best in town and say that your network is based on quality.

The greatest problem with tiered networks and all the variation research is that the punch line is always the same: We need to reengineer *all* clinical care to be higher quality and lower cost. Why? Because you can't actually move all the patients to the 25 percent best providers. They don't have the capacity, and the other 75 percent will be pissed.

Similarly, you can't take all the Medicare enrollees from Florida—where medical care utilization is apparently profligate, excessive, ineffectual, and larcenous—and move them to Minnesota for the nice, decent, conservative, and effective care that the variation folk tell us exists there. The elderly retire to Florida and other warm places with high-utilizing doctors, not to cold, northern Midwest states with conservative physicians. (Remember, before you "Ya, but" me, all these sweeping generalizations are backed by data that is on a per capita, risk-adjusted, and quality-adjusted basis.)

The real question is: Who will do the clinical transformation? Dr. Don Berwick (now administrator of the Centers for Medicare & Medicaid Services) and his valiant colleagues at the Institute for Healthcare Improvement have taught hundreds to make these changes. But we have hundreds of thousands to go.

We are seriously deluded if we expect doctors in ones and twos to spontaneously redesign their clinical practice as a result of exposure to tiered networks. They are more likely to complain their way to inclusion (or actively bamboozle their patients that the tiered networks are meaningless rubbish) without embracing the transformation required.

The clinical redesign requires a set of actors with the organizational, financial, and clinical scale as well as the resources to pull this off. Integrated delivery systems, large scale medical groups, and community hospitals that are constructively engaged with their medical staffs are the most likely candidates to lead appropriate clinical transformation that will reduce variation, improve quality and safety, and reduce the rate of cost increase.

Choice, Security, and Stuff

Life is filled with trade-offs,
and health care is no exception.

All economies and all health systems struggle with trade-offs among three key elements: choice, security, and stuff.

Choice

Choice is a manifestation of freedom. Americans love freedom and the choice that goes with it. We like choice of doctors, maybe even health plans, and we certainly don't want our choices limited by government fiat or managed care bureaucrats. When choice is constrained we get very cranky. We hate gatekeeper physicians; we detest pre-authorization; we can't stand limits on our use of expensive technology, even when it does more harm than good; and we go crazy when we are told we can't get what we want.

But sometimes we have too much choice for our health. We have a plethora of cheeseburger options (including a cheeseburger embedded in a Krispy Kreme doughnut—I am not making this up). Seniors have forty-five or more baffling Prescription Drug Plan choices in the Medicare Part D world. Doctors are free to perform any procedure they want if a consumer with cash asks for it. Sure, there is a wee thing called professional ethics, but the variation literature says there is a lot of excessive care based on provider preferences compared with best practices.

We have codified the health plan of the future as "you can have anything you want as long as you pay for it out of pocket." Certainly, we have some annoying bureaucratic hurdles, but generally you can get anything you want in health care, if your insurer—or more often now, you—are willing to pay for it.

All this choice comes at a cost. Not only are we being asked to pay more for choice in the form of premium sharing, co-payments, and deductibles, but because we have so much choice and we are unwilling to put limits either individually or collectively on our choices, health care is becoming increasingly unaffordable. Our freedom to choose in the short run may limit our choices in the long run. It's a bit like global warming.

Choice and Security

Unfettered choice is fueling cost escalation, and in the long run it will limit our ability to choose and undermine our health security. We see it in the growing numbers of uninsured: In the last decade, there has been a dramatic rise in the percentage of lower- and middle-income people without health insurance, largely due to the fact that small businesses and individuals increasingly can't afford health insurance.

We see it in the dire forecasts of how much money it takes to retire at age sixty-five to pay for out-of-pocket medical costs (currently estimated to be more than $250,000 per person). We see it in the rising number of medical-related bankruptcies. We see it most acutely in the Rust Belt industries where retired autoworkers have to gamble between health security and income security: For example, GM has offered a $140,000 buyout to workers with at least ten years on the job who are willing to walk away without continuing benefits.

We may see it in the public sector and local government, in particular, as the GASB (Governmental Accounting Standards Board) Statement #45 provisions begin to take effect and are eventually followed. (I am no accountant, but in a nutshell these provisions require state and local governments to make their unfunded retiree health benefit costs explicit on their balance sheets, starting with the largest entities on December 2006 and phasing in over the following three years.)

A senior financial services executive told me the effect would be to make every municipal bond in America a junk bond. He may be overstating the case, but these provisions—coupled to crushing state deficits since the recession—will surely put pressure on state and local governments to cut the generous retirement health benefits that schoolteachers, firefighters, and folks at the DMV have enjoyed. The private sector has already cut the obligations to future retirees; the public sector will likely follow. Many people chose the public sector for health and retirement security over income security—they may be disappointed in their choice.

Choice, Security, and Stuff

Until the great economic meltdown of 2008–09, rising health care costs and the looming threat of a retirement with inadequate or expensive benefits have not really limited our consumption of stuff. Low interest rates and high house prices buoyed an American's net worth (albeit on paper). We took out home equity lines to buy SUVs and other stuff. We consumers kept the American economy humming by borrowing money and getting bigger houses to store our stuff, as George Carlin so famously pointed out.

Health care may give us cause for concern in the future, but it has not seemed to cramp our style in the consumption of stuff in the present. And we don't seem that upset about it. This mystifies me. Economists will tell you that health benefits are part of total compensation (albeit tax-advantaged). Yet the lucky folks with health insurance think they get it free, or for the modest premium sharing. The reality is that working people with health insurance haven't had a wage increase in a decade because it all went to health benefits. Health care has limited their consumption of stuff, yet they blame the poor economy, not health care, for the problem. (See also the essay "In Search of the Next Economy," pp. 173–183.)

Looking Ahead

The trade-off among choice, security, and stuff will become more intense as we face a long, slow process of readjustment. In the Social Security debate, we elected the security part over the choice part and the prospect of more stuff that came with the private accounts.

In addition, consumers will be forced to select between a wide choice of providers and having more stuff as health care goes retail, making these trade-offs even more dramatic. In health care, we may start to value security over everything else—even if it means limiting our choices and getting a little less stuff.

The Fallacy of Excellence

*Superb inputs don't necessarily create
brilliant outcomes.*

"We have the best doctors and hospitals, and we have the best health care system in the world," I heard a Republican candidate for president say during the 2008 election. It rolled off his tongue very smoothly. The audience applauded, nodding quietly in assent. (I couldn't see them well enough—the camera was on him—but it felt like they were nodding.)

The candidate's statement struck me for two reasons. First, you don't hear it as often as you used to. Almost everyone from CEOs to presidents to policy wonkettes seems to think health care is broken, or in deep crisis. So when John McCain said it, it was kind of a nice retro moment, back to a time when almost everyone in America agreed with the three-step statement: best doctors, best hospitals, best health care system.

Second, what struck me was the fact that the audience applauded and nodded in agreement (in my mind's eye). In my rattling around American health care I see this all the time, among lay audiences, hospital board members, and a lot of business people. I have come to call it the "fallacy of excellence."

Only as Good as the System

There is a common perception that quality of inputs equals quality of performance and outcomes. Health care delivery has become

mind-bogglingly complicated, but we still like to cling to the simple, reassuring notion that if we have really well-trained doctors
and nurses and we put them in nice, new, sparkling buildings and
provide them with lots of new technology, we will always deliver
excellent care. I don't believe that. While having well-trained staff
and good facilities may be necessary conditions, they are far from
sufficient.

The health care glitterati agree that it takes a "system" to deliver
safe, reliable, high-quality, cost-effective care, from the very top
level of policy to the micro-organization of care. The general public
knows only too well the downside of a lack of systemness: from
the 47 million uninsured to the lack of coordination of caregivers
to the absence of a medical home. The public may know the system doesn't work, but it seems to me they still cling to the notion
that more is better, that good doctors and hospitals guarantee good
quality, and (maybe by inference) that higher costs and prices are
associated with excellence in outcomes.

I see this in the eyes of lay board members at hospital retreats.
I hear it in the questions from general audiences. And I see it in
folks whose eyes glaze over in disbelief that cost and quality may be
correlated inversely (namely, that high cost is associated with poor
quality, an assertion that has increasing evidence behind it from the
Dartmouth Atlas of Health Care to the Premier pay-for-performance
experiments with the Centers for Medicare & Medicaid Services).

If the public, doctors, and hospital trustees are aligned in the fallacy of excellence, that behavior may foreshadow a rocky road for
some important policy initiatives, such as:

Pay-for-performance (P4P) initiatives that reward efficiency. Increasingly the P4P movement will incorporate so-called efficiency measures
into its programs. This reinforces the notion that high-quality care
can also be of lower cost.

High-performance networks. Similarly, patients will be asked to
believe that lower-cost performers are also higher quality as they are
directed to so-called high-performing providers that are low-cost
and high-quality.

Center for comparative effectiveness. The Economic Stimulus
Act of 2008 created a national independent center to evaluate the

comparative effectiveness of new medical technologies and provide side-by-side analysis of the effectiveness of new technologies against existing therapies.

Changing the Mind-Set

In my humble opinion, even in the wake of a health reform debate, there needs to be a national campaign to educate the public (and maybe even the doctors and hospital trustees) that more is not better, that outcomes cannot be guaranteed by excellence of inputs, and that it takes a system at both the macro and micro levels to deliver good health care.

The Institute of Medicine has done a brilliant job of documenting the value of systemness in its path-breaking reports. But we need to popularize the message and educate the public that systems of care matter. Otherwise, the fallacy of excellence will dominate the public discourse on health care—from political campaign debates to hospital board retreats—and we will continue to spend more and get less than we should.

Explanation of Benefits

What explanation? What benefits?

Every health insurance company sends out these great little missives called explanation of benefits (EOBs). They are hilarious and the mother of all oxymorons because they don't explain anything and beneath all the obfuscation, you find out there are no benefits. While some enlightened insurers like Humana and Aetna put them on the Web (so you can be confused online as opposed to by snail mail), most of a health plan's communication to its members centers on these great little letters you get in the mail.

The EOBs come on flimsy paper and look suspiciously like a bill from one of those phony publishing companies. Then you open it and in big bold writing it says: "THIS IS NOT A BILL." (So why are they sending it?) You read on: It's a pre-bill, you are going to get a bill, this is just not it, quite yet. But it does help to get a little story in spreadsheet form as to why your health insurance is not covering your health care services. Oh, by the way, you get this a long time after you have had the service they talk about in the EOB. Beautiful.

My family gets lots of these letters, and because we are dealing with several insurers, we get to sample the quality of communication of many health plans and their members. The EOB is just part of the way health insurers communicate with their members. Utilization management sends out great little form letters, too. My wife got one that said the diagnostic service she had on June 17 was deemed medically necessary, but it went on (in bold capital letters) to say:

"THIS CERTIFICATION IS BASED ON THE INFORMATION PROVIDED, AND IS OF MEDICAL NECESSITY ONLY AND IS NOT A GUARANTEE THAT HEALTH BENEFITS WILL BE PAID." The letter was sent June 18.

It's a Secret

Another exchange between my wife and the customer service department of a major national insurer yielded the following insanity. My wife wanted to move her regular source of care from one group practice to another in our local area. She asked two very simple questions of the health plan: Who is available, and what would be the cost? After going through several layers of supervisors, she was told: "We can't tell you that, it's a secret." Basically, to give away cost to an enrollee in a high-deductible plan is to give away discounts and negotiated rates. It's a secret. I told this story to a group of benefit managers of large employers, and one benefit manager jokingly agreed in frustration: "They told us it was a secret, too."

The point is this: We are now a decade into the so-called consumer market, yet health insurers are still wedded to convoluted, bureaucratic communication that obfuscates their responsibilities and simply leaves the consumer with the financial gotcha (after the care is long since consumed and forgotten), when the provider finally tracks the patient down for the "amount you owe," known affectionately as patient responsibility. The absolute worst gotcha is recision of benefits, where the health insurers wriggle out of any financial responsibility on legal technicalities when patients have racked up big bills for lengthy illnesses. Insurers may have a legal case, but do they have a moral case? (Luckily, health reform has made this illegal, except in cases of blatant fraud.)

The Obfuscation Plan

There are two major implications of the EOB morass. First is that health insurers and providers alike have a long way to go in creating true transparency on cost and quality. To have truly informed consumer decision making requires that providers and insurers coordinate their communication to clearly tell the patient what it will cost patients at the time the patient has to make the decision to have the service or not. The health care system fails miserably on this simplest of all market tests: You know the price before you buy.

New models like "Carol" (a Web-based market maker that enlists providers and plans in a consumer-friendly comparison shopping environment) hold some promise, but their penetration is infinitesimal, and there is really no reason for providers and plans to want to make it easier for consumers when the gotcha model is so spectacularly effective in obfuscating how much things really cost.

The second big implication is at the policy level. Until their more recent woes due to health reform, health insurers have had a great run financially since 2000. They remain incredibly unpopular with the American public in national surveys of trust in health care. They showed a willingness to make important concessions in the policymaking process with regard to expansion of coverage for all Americans at both the state and national level, even as they continue to be demonized by the Obama administration. This is not the "Harry and Louise" crowd of the 1990s health reform debate.

Nevertheless, health insurers became the targets of punitive regulation. Insurers got guaranteed issuance, rate setting, medical-loss requirements, prohibitions on recision, marketing constraints, Medicare Advantage cuts, and a whole host of state regulation (where the real powers to regulate currently lie).

Part of the reason insurers are in the crosshairs is that they are not seen by providers or patients as adding much value. We don't want single-payer, government-run health care, but we don't like the private-sector pluralism much, either. Health insurers have been asked to justify their benefit to society, and they'd better have a good explanation.

On the building blocks
of health reform

The 20 Percent Solution

Just spend MORE!

I was always taught that America spends too much on health care already; therefore, we should be able to reallocate resources to cover the uninsured, increase wellness and health promotion activities, and improve the quality of clinical care. That may well be true, but as we have found out over the last thirty years, it is simply impossible to achieve in the American political context. Reallocation means that someone's income has to go down, and that's not going to happen.

In my rattling around American health care, I have come to realize that the only thing that unites doctors, hospitals, drug companies, the elderly, academic medical centers, the safety net, the public health community, health plans, and medical equipment manufacturers is that they all want more money spent on them. So that's the answer: Let's build a coalition of all the actors who want MORE. Can you imagine drug companies, doctors, hospitals, and AARP unleashing their enormous lobbying power, marching arm in arm to the Capitol singing "Kumbaya"?

Here's how it would work. Let's assume we are spending $1.5 trillion on health care this year and it's about 15 percent of a $10 trillion economy. The new MORE coalition demands that we increase health spending immediately by 20 percent, approximately $300 billion a year, and we make it a national goal to have health care account for 20 percent of GNP within five years (or $2 trillion in today's dollars). Hey, we'll be there anyway in 2020, so why not start now? We need the practice.

How would we spend the money? We would pay people to eliminate disparities and variation in health care. We would cover prescription drugs. We would improve long-term care. We would cover the uninsured. We would invest in public health infrastructure, and we would embark on redesigning health care finance and delivery from the ground up for when we Baby Boomers really need it, ten years from now.

If we spend two-thirds of the increment on labor costs, that's $200 billion worth of new jobs. You could have half a million jobs at $100,000 a year, 2 million at $50,000, and 2 million at $25,000. Or you could give invasive cardiologists a big raise.

Okay, you've spotted the problem: Where does the money come from? Let's assume there are 100 million tax-paying households (there are more, but I don't know how to work the calculator on my laptop, so the math is easier this way). Ultimately, they pay—whether in taxes, as part of wages, or as out-of-pocket costs. It comes to about $15,000 per household already spent on health care by all the actors (business, government, and households); we are just asking for $3,000 more per household per year. The top third of households by income would pay for the bottom third ($6,000 versus zero). Seems fair. What else would you spend it on, anyway, Britney Spears albums and dinner out?

Crazy idea, eh? No crazier than spending $1.5 trillion on a system of uneven quality and huge disparities, having more than 40 million uninsured, and having few people doing anything meaningful about it.

Tax Policy as Health Policy

*Tax cuts have limited our nation's ability
to provide insurance to the indigent,
cover medications for the elderly,
and keep foundering health systems afloat.*

Policy wonks love to talk about alternative ways to cover the uninsured, exciting new quality and patient safety initiatives, meaningful pay-for-performance systems, and so forth. All of this is completely irrelevant. The single biggest issue that affects health care in the short term and the long term is tax policy. When the rich among us received a big tax cut, it virtually dictated massive state budget crises and a rise in the uninsured. The massive federal deficit that the tax cuts created constrains meaningful expansion of health care to the uninsured and will require Medicare beneficiaries to dig deep into their own pockets to pay the premiums for the old Medicare Part B and for the new drug benefit. If we make the tax cuts permanent, we are sealing the fate of many of the vulnerable elderly and the uninsured.

Why is tax policy so important, and how do we differ from other countries and health systems? Here are some thoughts:

American health care financing is increasingly regressive. Health care premiums are a regressive form of taxation for a social good: Everyone pays the same regardless of income. Indeed, when you factor in the corporate tax deductibility of health insurance premiums, well-compensated executives getting health insurance from their company are receiving a nice tax-free benefit; the higher paid they are, the more the benefit is worth in net terms.

Admittedly, while Social Security tax maxes out at $87,000 of income (2003 ceiling), the Medicare tax of 2.9 percent (half paid by employee, half by employer, all by the self-employed) is a flat tax with no ceiling. It's still not a progressive tax. Million-dollar earners are paying $29,000 toward Medicare—a big number to be sure. But consider this: According to distinguished Canadian health economist Robert Evans, the top decile of income earners in Canada are spending on average 10 percent of their total income to support the health system in Canada through progressive general taxation. There are actually a few million-dollar earners in Canada, such as Wayne Gretzky, Jim Carrey, William Shatner, and Michael J. Fox (most of whom actually pay taxes in the United States—but play along with me for purposes of exposition). Those same million-dollar Canadian earners would pay about $100,000 toward the Canadian Medicare system. Admittedly, they don't have to pay any health premiums, just taxes. So for the sake of fairness, you have to add to the American executive's bill about $10,000 in premiums for a family (nice coverage, too). Bearing in mind it's a tax-free benefit, and while it really is part of total compensation, many folks think health care provided by their employer is free. Suppose also that there is some portion of general taxation earmarked for health care purposes like Medicaid—let's say 2 percent of earnings (or $20,000). We're still only at $59,000.

Remember that Canadians spend 10 percent of their GDP on health care, a number that has been flat throughout Jean Chretien's terms as prime minister (ironically because rich Canadians wanted a tax cut, which meant constraining the total health budget). We in the United States spend close to 15 percent of our GDP. So it is logical to assume that Canadian-style progressive tax financing (even using American top rates of tax, which are not that much different) would create a tax burden for the hypothetical rich American in a single-payer system of about $150,000 as opposed to the $59,000 they currently pay. This is crude analysis; I'd love to see a real policy wonk do it properly. It's hard to figure out. But do you know who *has* figured it out? Rich people. That's why the rich are more likely to vote Republican, and more likely to be against single-payer policies (unless they are rich people from Boston, New York, Seattle, or San Francisco—the civilized world as we now know it).

The values are shifting away from social solidarity. Health care systems can survive only if there is a massive transfer of income from rich people to poor people and from well people to sick people. Even the American system does this, because allocating health care solely on the ability to pay is barbaric. But as the medical concierge and VIP medicine crowd are finding out, there is a very good reason for providers to want a cross-subsidy to the poor sick from the healthy rich. Why? There aren't enough rich people to go around. A lot of doctors think consumers should pay for all care out of their pockets. These doctors believe that their waiting rooms are full of malingering riffraff with minor boring conditions, and that if ability to pay were factored in, their waiting rooms would be full of rich people with interesting diseases. Wrong. Cross-subsidy matters, not just for social solidarity purposes but because it is good for providers.

My colleagues at Harris Interactive have asked the public about their values and beliefs. A classic question sums it up: Do you agree or disagree with the following statement? "The higher someone's income is, the more that he or she should expect to pay in taxes to cover the cost of people who are less well off and are heavy users of medical services." In 1991, on the eve of a Clinton presidency, 66 percent of Americans agreed with the statement. By 2003, in the midst of the Bush administration, only 51 percent agreed with the statement. It says a lot about the erosion of social solidarity that has occurred in twelve years.

Tax credits for the rich and poor. A centerpiece of Bush administration policy (and one echoed by Republicans since that time) has been tax credits and tax-advantaged medical savings accounts for rich and poor alike. But if you have mastered first-grade arithmetic, you will know that a tax credit or a tax-advantaged plan is worth more to rich people who pay high taxes than to poor people who pay little or no taxes.

The undeserving rich. America rightfully honors its million-dollar earners; you come here with nothing and you make a lot. America has been very, very good to Arnold, and Ariana, and Wayne Gretzky, and me. But what made America the greatest country in the world is not that it had the lowest taxes but that it was a country that offered freedom and opportunity in a place that was safe, fair, and compassionate. Giving massive tax breaks to Paris Hilton so she can buy more Prada handbags doesn't strike me as consistent with American values. Better she has fewer handbags and we have less uninsured.

First Class

In the United States, the rich pay proportionately less
of the health care bill while receiving better care.

We have a first-class health care system. It works pretty well for people in first class, but if you are in coach you might not be so happy.

Class (by this I mean socioeconomic status) is increasingly the predictor of health care outcomes, service, and satisfaction. And here's the really good part: If you are in first class, you pay less of your income for health care than if you are in coach.

The Role of Class in Health

A number of recent studies are reinforcing a point that we have known for a very long time: Socioeconomic class is a powerful predictor of disparities in health care treatment and outcome, even when adjusted for access. Here are two recent examples, quoted directly from the news feeds or the study abstract:

Study of Disability Rates in the United States

Respondents ages 55 to 64 with annual incomes of less than the federal poverty level—at the time, $8,259 for an individual—were six times more likely to have disabilities that limited activities such as walking, climbing stairs and lifting objects than those in the same age group with incomes of $60,000 or more. The study also found that the rate of disabilities continued to decrease among respondents ages 55 to 64 as annual incomes increased higher than $60,000.

Study authors said the disparity did not result only because of more limited access to health care. . . . [University of California, Berkeley professor and lead author] Meredith Minkler . . . said: "Social class is a tremendously important risk factor for disability." (M. Minkler, E. Fuller-Thomson, and J. Guralnik, "Gradient of Disability across the Socioeconomic Spectrum in the United States," *New England Journal of Medicine* 355 [Aug. 17, 2006]: 695–703)

U.S. and British Comparisons

The U.S. population in late middle age is less healthy than the equivalent British population for diabetes, hypertension, heart disease, myocardial infarction, stroke, lung disease and cancer. . . . This conclusion [controls] for a standard set of behavioral risk factors, including smoking, overweight, obesity and alcohol drinking.

Among those aged 55 to 64 years, diabetes prevalence is twice as high in the United States and only one fifth of this difference can be explained by a common set of risk factors. These differences are not solely driven by the bottom of the [socioeconomic status] distribution. In many diseases, the top of the SES distribution is less healthy in the United States as well. (J. Banks, M. Marmot, Z. Oldfield, and J. Smith, "Disease and Disadvantage in the United States and in England," *Journal of the American Medical Association* 295 [2006]: 2037–2045)

The dramatic differences across socioeconomic class reported by these studies are not just about access to health care or insurance coverage. They point to the fundamental role of class as a determinant of health. But obviously, these results are further compounded by the well-documented effects on one's health by both health insurance status and race and ethnicity.

For example, analysis by the Commonwealth Fund has shown that among working people, only 5 percent of those in the top income quintile (roughly $90,000-plus in household income) are uninsured, whereas 52 percent in the lowest income quintile (households earning less than $20,000) lack insurance. The most dramatic recent increase in uninsured rates is among those households earning between $20,000 and $35,000 (the second and third quintile of income). All of these effects are even worse when race and ethnicity are added to the mix, as the Institute of Medicine's 2003 report *Unequal Treatment* carefully documents. (By the way, the U.S.-U.K. study focused solely on white patients, partially I believe to head off the old canard of international comparison studies, namely that the United States is different because of our more heterogeneous population.)

The bottom line of these studies is that socioeconomic status matters a great deal and that there are real smart scientists who believe there are neurophysiological processes at work affecting human biology that have to do with stress and degree of control. In reviewing the U.S.-U.K. study with a British journalist from the *Financial Times* of London, I speculated that we all work too hard in the United States, and the poorer you are and the fewer educational opportunities you have, the harder you have to work. Maybe we should all put down our brooms or our BlackBerrys and go to the pub—we might be a lot healthier.

Class and Payment

Still, I want to link the concept of class to the broader question of who pays for health care, because we have a unique set of circumstances in the United States in which the income distribution is getting ever more extreme (the very rich are getting very much richer) at the same time that we have health care financing policies that are regressive in their funding.

High-deductible health plans (HDHPs) in general, and health savings accounts (HSAs) in particular, are regressive forms of payment (rich people pay a smaller share of income to health care than poor people). As I have estimated before, a million-dollar-a-year earner in Canada would pay $150,000 in taxes toward health care, while a million-dollar earner in the United States would pay about $58,000 in taxes and premiums toward health care.

That is why single-payer schemes, such as a California proposal in 2006, are an assault to the status quo. The proposed legislation would have been paid by an 8 percent payroll tax and a 3 percent individual income tax, probably doubling the overall health care bill for those million-dollar earners. Obviously, only a few hundred thousand folk in America make over $1 million a year, but we all think we will: If we can't go the Princeton–Stanford–venture capital route, we are betting on the NBA, hip hop, or no-limit Texas hold 'em to get us to the bling.

The ongoing battle over Obamacare will center on whether the middle class associates itself politically with the top or the bottom of the income distribution. Bear in mind that only slim majorities of national or California voters are willing to pay any more in taxes for health care, and that the support evaporates after about $200 per year in additional taxes. It will be interesting to watch.

A Modest Proposal

Here's my little idea for modifying Obamacare. What if we took the best of the right and left? High-deductible health plans are cheaper because they don't cover everything, and when people have to pay out of pocket they use less. (This may be good, bad, or ugly depending on what care is forgone, but many of us believe it is generally bad or ugly—causing people, particularly low-income people, to postpone needed preventive services or not comply with treatment.) The reason HDHPs are cheaper is not because of the tax advantage of HSAs but because of the high deductible.

We should cover preventive services and chronic care medications on a comprehensive basis (as specified in the Patient Protection and Affordable Care Act). We should have incentives for patients to be mindful of cost (not just drugs). And we should make the financing system a bit more progressive than regressive if we want to mitigate some of the worst effects of class.

So here goes: Everyone gets a basic preventive package covered on a first-dollar basis, and everyone gets a $10,000 per household deductible catastrophic health plan (premium sharing would be based on income). Everything in the middle (the $10,000 in patient spending) is on a sliding co-insurance scale where the lowest-income folk pay zero co-insurance and the top-income folk pay a 100 percent co-insurance rate.

According to recent data from the Census Bureau, 23.7 million households (some 20 percent) earn over $100,000 in household income, and 2.3 million households make over $250,000. Those top 1 percent or 2 percent earners would pay a larger share of premium, the taxes necessary to cover the premium subsidy to the poor, and up to $10,000 out of pocket, making hospitals, doctor visits, and elective surgery a bit more of a retail experience.

Oh . . . and we probably should be using after-tax dollars, not pre-tax dollars, in a health savings account.

By making the affluent, well-educated, savvy consumers pay more for first class, we might even get the effects promised by the consumer-directed advocates, such as more questioning of the prices charged by providers. Enlightened employers like the University of California have some elements that point in this direction, such as income-based premium sharing: Janitors pay less toward health care than tenured professors, but that is a small step toward addressing the disparities created by socioeconomic class.

Before the rich readers go up in arms about socialism and income redistribution being dangerous and seditious, let me point out it is better for you than the single-payer alternative, which is, by its nature, an even more massive transfer of income from rich to poor.

It is important for all of us in health care to remember that class matters. It is always good to be in first class, but way too many of us never get the upgrade.

Care, Not Coverage

Maybe our focus on insurance is wrong.

We should cover the uninsured. You hear that a lot. We have been saying it for forty years. It happened under Obamacare, but it may get rolled back.

Even in the roaring '90s when the economy was rocking and rolling, when really rich Americans earned a lot and paid a lot in taxes, when we had a popular Democratic president, and when we had a government surplus, we did not cover the uninsured. Maybe we don't want to. Maybe it is just too expensive now. Maybe we can't be bothered, what with Iraq and the war on terrorism and global warming and all.

Nevertheless, covering the uninsured became popular again in 2007. Politicians, from governors to mayors to even presidential candidates, speechified about covering the uninsured. We even got further than that and passed some legislation.

Massachusetts offers an interesting state-level experiment in which everyone, both employer and individual, is compelled to participate. In Massachusetts, health care insurance is both a right and an obligation: You have the right to expect health insurance coverage, but you have an obligation to pay something for it. (Note that it doesn't seem providers have to sacrifice anything—they just get more insured patients.)

We continue to watch Massachusetts very closely, but can we learn from the experiment and apply it elsewhere? As I point out to my Boston buddies, we have more uninsured in California than they have people in Massachusetts, so the problem is of a different scale in California or Texas.

California Coverage

Speaking of California, the residents of that state had a wave of initiatives washing over them in the mid-2000s. They have universal coverage in San Francisco. (Actually it is not coverage, because according to the mayor it is not insurance, because insurance would be challenged on Employee Retirement Income Security Act [ERISA] preemption grounds, and challenging ERISA is like challenging big tobacco: You don't go there. So it may look like insurance—you pay a premium and you get covered services—but it is not insurance, okay?)

At least in San Francisco the bureaucrats have run the numbers past actuaries and come up with a very rich benefits package for only $201 per month. How can they do it? They're presuming that all providers will spontaneously accept Medicaid rates. Other plans have been floated in California, including everything from single-payer alternatives to employee mandates (the so-called SB2 ballot initiative that was shot down).

Again in California, Kaiser Permanente developed an ambitious and logical proposal to cover the state's uninsured by requiring all taxpayers to participate in some form of coverage. Those who are ineligible for existing public and private programs or cannot afford them (below 300 percent of the federal poverty level) would be funded through a mix of payroll and provider taxes at a total additional cost of $7.5 billion.

And in 2007 Gov. Arnold Schwarzenegger declared that universal health care coverage was his top priority. The governor's plan was to be commended for the "shared sacrifice" that it requires. Government (especially the federal government) had to give some, and state taxpayers had to give some. Businesses with more than ten employees had to "pay or play" (provide insurance or pay into a state pool). Other individuals, including those who work for small businesses, had to buy at least a catastrophic coverage plan. And most interestingly, providers were taxed (4 percent for hospitals and 2 percent for doctors) in recognition that their uncompensated care burden would be reduced by expanded coverage and improved Medicaid reimbursement. All oxen were gored in the process, which is a good thing.

Ironically, this plan from a Republican governor (Schwarzenegger), modeled as it was after the plan of another Republican governor (Mitt Romney), is eerily prescient of Obamacare.

This and all plans say very little about how health care will become more affordable or how costs will be contained in the long run. But overall, it represents an emerging consensus that health care is both a right and an obligation. You have the right to expect some access to health care, and you have the obligation to participate in paying for it. It's easy to say, but the hard part is figuring out who pays for what.

Focusing on Care

The Patient Protection and Affordable Care Act (PPACA) is now law, expanding Medicare coverage by 16 million people and offering private insurance through exchanges.

But maybe we need to change the focus from coverage to care. For example, giving people an insurance card helps only if a provider accepts both them and the card. Try, for example, finding an OB/GYN in California if you are on Medi-Cal. We might be better off training a whole cadre of nurse practitioners to create universal prenatal and well-baby care as a government-funded service, like K–12 education. People can always buy additional insurance if they want more than the basic program. (The massive expansion in funding for community clinics in PPACA is, in part, in recognition that providing an insurance card will not guarantee access to care, particularly primary care.)

A further benefit of focusing on care delivery, not coverage, would be reducing the absolutely staggering costs of administering the eligibility requirements for complex, means-tested programs involving moms and kids in poverty. My favorite statistic is that there are 1,900 people employed in Los Angeles County who do nothing but fill out Medi-Cal eligibility forms for county residents at a union-mandated productivity target of two such forms per day! We should give these employees white coats and have them go to schools to immunize kids and teach them about the perils of a fast-food diet. Oh, and if we extended the universal care system to all kids, eligibility would be easy; if you are a kid, you get care: no coverage, no forms, no questions.

Mandated Competition

We have to get over this freedom thing
and stop cheating.

Americans hate mandates. Mandates to cover specific diseases and conditions drive health insurance costs up. Mandates to provide open access to emergency rooms sink geographically undesirable hospitals. Mandates to collect, collate, and communicate data create burdensome administrative chores. Now we are going to add more mandates in health care. We are talking about all Americans being mandated to buy health insurance. We are also talking about insurers being mandated to offer insurance and not have the freedom to walk away from risks they don't like.

But while many health care folks hate mandates there are also a lot of mandates they really like. Doctors of all stripes like the mandates that you have to be a doctor or a certain type of "ologist" to do certain procedures and tasks and access the income streams associated with it. Hospitals like the mandate that they are the place where certain procedures can be done. Employers like the mandate that because of the Employee Retirement Income Security Act they can't be mandated by states to do things. Sweet.

We have to put up with other mandates in our lives, like income tax, parking tickets, bridge tolls, paying admission to ball games, and so on. We are not mandated to vote, like the Australians (maybe we should be—then look out).

Coverage Mandates

Let's be clear: There is no such thing as voluntary universal coverage anywhere in the world. By the same token, while many countries including Japan, Germany, and Holland have mandated insurance that achieves almost complete universal coverage, similar schemes in America would not yield anything close to universal coverage. Why? Because we would cheat.

We have to have car insurance and many of us don't. We have to have children in order to claim children as dependents on our income tax, but until some smart aleck at the IRS started asking for the Social Security numbers of the kids, more than 7 million nonexistent kids were claimed as dependents. We listen to National Public Radio and we never pledge. So even liberals cheat. That doesn't mean that mandates in health care don't make a lot of sense; it just means we have to worry about enforcing them in a nation of cheaters.

Part of the reason cheaters cheat when it comes to car insurance and possibly health insurance is that the cheaters either can't afford it or the consequences of not having insurance are less dire than buying it. As Judge Harry Low, former California health insurance commissioner, once famously said, "You don't need insurance unless you have assets to protect."

I favor mandates for individuals. But I also favor employer mandates, starting with the largest and moving down to all employers over time. Eventually we will meet in the German middle where health care is paid by a payroll tax (half employer-paid, half employee-paid) with a ceiling on total payment close to our current Federal Insurance Contributions Act ceiling on income, because upper-income folk don't like progressive taxation.

Issuance Mandates

Health insurers should not just pick and choose worthy risks. There are precedents internationally for risk-adjustment factors that even out the adverse selection effects on insurers (see my essay on Australia entitled "Aussie, Aussie, Aussie," pp. 131–136).

Cream skimming by insurers that leaves vulnerable families destitute is more of a crime than inadequately adjusted adverse selection experienced by a multibillion-dollar insurer.

Provider Mandates

At a meeting of the World Healthcare Congress, a New Zealand doctor was asked how that country achieved virtually universal adoption of electronic health records (EHRs) by that nation's primary care doctors (compared with approximately 20 percent of primary care doctors in the United States). In his wonderfully quiet and clipped New Zealand accent he said: "The government won't pay you unless you have one." Brilliant.

Now, I am sympathetic to the economic plight of American primary care doctors who currently earn approximately half of the pay of their British brethren. So here's my idea: Tell doctors that they can't bill Medicare unless they have an EHR by 2015 and give them a tax credit to put one in. (The Economic Stimulus Act funding of EHRs and the meaningful use provisions create a mandate [or carrot and stick] to install an EHR.) While we are at it, we should have mandatory public reporting of standardized costs and quality metrics by all providers.

Patient Mandates

We slothful consumers should not get off the hook. Everyone should be mandated to complete a health risk appraisal (HRA) before enrolling in any health insurance plan. No HRA, no coverage. Our co-payment should rise if we are not in compliance with our treatment plan. And we should all be mandated to submit to arbitration before we get to sue our health plan, our doctor, or our employer over health issues.

Then let's have it in a good old-fashioned market, competing head-to-head on the basis of cost, quality, and value. And let's not whine about it.

Rich Man, Poor Man

*How much health care
will rich people buy for poor people?
And do the poor really want it?*

At the core of the health reform debate is the desire to get everyone covered. Sure, we want it to be affordable and sustainable economically; we want value (quality and access for the dollar); and we want consistent, reliable, evidence-based care. This is all good stuff, but at the root of health reform is the idea that we are going to find a way for everyone to have coverage. For the coverage to be universal, rich people will have to subsidize poor people, and well people will have to subsidize sick people. But how much coverage should the rich buy for the poor, or the well for the sick? As the debate unfolded, the exact amount of the bill being presented to the rich and the well became clearer.

I have argued before that coverage is not necessarily the right way to do it. Maybe we should just provide care directly to people who don't have insurance through a publicly funded delivery system (think community clinics on steroids, with catastrophic insurance for very serious illness). But, since that idea goes over like a lead balloon, policymakers came back to the notion that everyone should have an insurance card.

Drawbacks to Universal Coverage

Here are a few observations about the economic perversity of this quest to give everyone a card.

Deal or no deal. Obscure academic researchers have argued that the current health insurance system forces working families to consume more health insurance (and health care) than they would really want if they had the option of using the money for something else. Imagine if the conversation went something like this between a working-class person with insurance and a cardiologist suggesting balloon angioplasty for marginally indicated coronary artery disease.

"Well Mr. Johnson, we could do a procedure that won't make much difference, for $20,000 or so, or . . . you could have a new truck. What would you like to do?"

Alternatively, consider the ninety-two-year-old man who was offered the choice of spending his last five days in an ICU or leaving his family $100,000. What would he do?

Obviously, we don't want health care to be quite so crass, but I exaggerate to make the point that some of the uninsured might not want as much coverage (or care) as you might think. Consider the young immortal segment of the uninsured: the twenty-something kids who have left the nest and are in their "barista, perpetual self-discovery, extended adolescence" phase. Recently, when a major health plan ran proprietary focus groups with these immortals, probing them on how high-deductible health insurance could cost them as little as they pay for cell phone service for a month, the response from the barista crowd was shock and awe:

"Dude, you've gotta be f$%%8 kidding me, my phone is my life, I live on this phone, what do I need health insurance for? Give up my phone for health insurance, you people must be smoking something, Dude, get a life. . . ."

Yet, we seem intent on giving these kids a card that covers everything, and one that they may be forced by law to buy. All for considerably more than their cell phone costs them.

Piling on the rich. Every few years we gorge ourselves to excess, celebrate the overpaid, and then demonize them for the very excesses that we so envied and admired. It was our collective envy for *Lifestyles of the Rich and Famous* that crashed during the dot-com bust, only to be replaced by *Cribs, The Real Housewives of Orange County* (New York, Atlanta, and New Jersey), *Sweet Sixteen,* and all the other "everything Paris Hilton" reality shows that document in popular culture (in painstaking detail) how money and taste are inversely correlated.

Then comes AIG and Bernie Madoff . . . bastards. Yet, these are the very people we are relying on to pay for universal coverage: the top 1 percent of households. The vapid, overindulged, spoiled, gilded, and overcompensated. We are counting on them.

The Obama administration has made clear from the beginning that those making over $250,000 would pay way more to redress the imbalances of the Bush years. It was a simple, compelling political proposition: The rich made out well for a long time, so tax the rich, and only the rich, a bit more. John McCain tried to portray $250,000 as more of an upper-middle-class threshold of income, not rich. (And to be fair, in many metro areas, a couple of high school principals or a police inspector with overtime and his nurse-with-shift-differential wife could eke their way into the $250,000-plus range in good years.)

But the real deal is in the top 1 percent of income: That is where the money must come from. For example, in the state of California, exactly 146,000 households (those with an adjusted gross income of $500,000 per annum) account for 25 percent of California's revenues when you include state income tax and capital gains tax. These folks will be asked to pay for the expansion in coverage at the federal level, and in the long run, they may have the tax deductibility of their rich coverage rolled back, as well as their itemized deductions.

It's all good. The rich can take it; after all, what's a Mercedes here and there? Problem is that the next couple of years may be a bit rocky for the high fliers, so paying for health care will inevitably require broader and deeper sacrifice to the average American household.

Relying on the average American household. Median household income in 2010 will be about $50,000, while average health expenditures per household is north of $18,000. Do you believe the average household would really want to spend a third of its income on health care if they had to pay their fair share? That is why health care affordability was such a popular political stance. But affordability to the public means they were going to get something back, like a check, or a big discount on what they pay for health care. But actually they will have to pay more for the system to get everyone covered because we probably don't have enough rich people to go around to pay for everyone else.

Suggestions for Coverage

How do we fix this all? I supported universal coverage, and I believe the rich should subsidize the poor, and the well the sick. I support mandates, but I think it would be a big mistake if we try to push through a "same big card for all" plan that requires people to purchase more health coverage and care than they would want individually or collectively. So here are some elements to think about:

Strip down the basic plan. As we design regulations for insurance exchanges, we should provide a basic benefit plan that uses a combination of benefit design and restricted network that makes it affordable for people mandated to buy it, particularly cell phone–wielding baristas. The Australians figured out how to suck young folk into private insurance: Make them pay higher premiums for every year after thirty that they postpone joining private coverage.

Consider care and coverage mixes for affordability. The combination of a subsidized primary care delivery system for lower-income people and catastrophic coverage might be more affordable than a comprehensive insurance card with pathetic reimbursement that no provider will take. (There may still be opportunities to pilot such models as disproportionate share hospital payments recede.)

Find ways to give people an option to consume cheaper, almost-as-good alternatives, and let them keep the difference. What's so crazy about saying to people: Do you want all this health care, or would you rather have other social services like education, housing, transportation, jobs, or income support? My guess is people will say: Keep your health care; give me the truck.

Compel participation in, but not overconsumption of, health care services. Shared responsibility for health care is a good thing. All residents should be compelled to participate, and they should be subsidized if they truly can't afford it. But we should not be compelled to overconsume ineffective health care services.

Consider that a lot of countries use cost sharing as a deterrent. Countries like Spain, Holland, and France maintain the illusion of cost sharing (even though some like France end up publicly subsidizing all of the low-income patients' out-of-pocket costs) because they want their citizens to have some skin in the game, particularly for middle- and upper-income people. We may need to have this as a national principle—but look out, autoworkers.

We can get health reform, but we need to be prepared to give something in the process. The danger is that we assume that we can have universal, comprehensive coverage for all Americans with exactly the same delivery system for everyone, just like the one we have now, and nobody has to change anything because fundamentally it is brilliant the way it is. And Paris Hilton will pay for all of it. I don't think so.

*On politics and policy
in the moment—
a window on the time*

The 2008 Election

Rising consumer costs, retiring Baby Boomers,
and Medicare reform will push health care
to center stage in 2008.

Author's note: *This section of the book includes five essays that reflect the tone of a particular point in time. They are published here without further editing to reflect fully the thinking of the moment. For example, the following essay was written in the summer of 2004, immediately before George W. Bush was elected for a second term.*

The presidential election of 2008 will be the most important event in the history of American health care. While health care is always a hot political topic in any election year (including this one), it is going to be absolutely critical in 2008, no matter what the outcome is this November. Why? Here are a few reasons.

Consumer-deflected health care. There is considerable momentum behind the move to shift costs to consumers, and despite consumers' bitching, there is little to stop the trend. Health costs for employers have been rising at double-digit rates for almost five years, and employers have finally developed the backbone necessary to stick it to their employees. Because everyone is worried about having his or her job outsourced to India, the employee is eating the cost shift, albeit reluctantly. There is no reason this trend cannot continue for three or four more years, but it is not a long-run solution. Just imagine how cranky we will all be in 2008 when we are paying, out of our own pockets, thousands of dollars a year for health care.

The Baby Boomers confront retirement security. The oldest Baby Boomers will turn sixty in 2007, and it is quite likely that this will be exactly the time when the penny finally drops for them: They have not saved enough money for retirement. Most importantly, they will realize that they don't have the close to $200,000 actuaries tell us they will need for out-of-pocket health care costs. Most of us will have to work forever; we will all become limo drivers in Boca Raton hauling other Baby Boomers around.

From a soccer-mom agenda to a retirement security agenda. The baby boom has transformed every institution it has touched, from the elementary schools of the '50s to the colleges of the '60s and '70s and the workplace of the '80s and '90s. We boomers are used to being accommodated and being in charge. While Clinton rode to political power partly on the strength of the soccer moms' support, the sixty-somethings of the future will be a powerful political force. Will they anticipate their looming retirement politically in 2008, or will they wait until it is almost too late (2012)? Medicare won't go bust, they say, until 2017—and maybe further out if you believe some of the optimists. But there is no question that a massive cohort of selfish, insecure, worried, narcissistic Baby Boomers will expect to be catered to, and I will be at the head of the line.

The fallout from Medicare reform. The new Medicare benefit will be the status quo in 2008. Unless it is overturned or substantially modified in the interim, the elderly will have real experience with discount cards and doughnut holes, and the pharmaceutical industry will have many of its blockbusters off patent (either generic or over the counter). The 2008 election will be a referendum on the effectiveness of Medicare reform.

What will be the outcome? I don't know. But I hope we have a real debate about American values of fairness; innovation; and economic, personal, and fiscal responsibility. Most importantly, by 2008 we will need to have a national debate about the fundamental and total redesign of health care delivery and the system to finance it. Because one thing we can't ignore is the reality of 2022, when the peak of the baby boom hits sixty-five and all of us will be sitting around in nursing homes singing "I got you, Babe." We can't extrapolate that demographic into the current health care system.

The New American Compromise

We can cover the uninsured,
but can we contain costs?

Author's note: *This essay was written in late 2007, not long before the first of the presidential primaries.*

In the 1980s and 1990s, an American compromise called managed competition was the dominant force behind health reform. Born from the ideas of Alain Enthoven at Stanford University, the theory laid out a path where consumers picked plans when they were well and lived with the consequences of their decision when they were sick. Integrated delivery systems organized in an HMO model competed for business on the basis of cost and quality, and cost-conscious consumers had real incentives to select low-cost plans; otherwise, they paid hundreds of dollars a month for more expensive (and usually broader choice) alternatives.

Managed competition was the basis for health reform initiatives in California in the 1980s and was really the intellectual foundation for all health reform efforts in the 1990s, including the ill-fated Clinton health plan. Managed competition worked best in a framework of universal coverage. Everyone was to be in a plan, and plan sponsors (such as employers or government) as well as individual consumers would have a marketplace of choices at the plan level or the integrated delivery system level. Kaiser-like entities would then compete on a value basis within a framework of universal coverage.

I always kind of liked the idea because it reconciled issues of cost, quality, and access, and I felt it was a genuinely American compromise between top-down control and consumer choice.

Shared Sacrifice

There is a "new American compromise" being forged. Emerging from the Romney and Schwarzenegger political aberrations (popular Republican governors in strongly Democratic states), the new American compromise makes universal coverage the primary goal. It is to be achieved through shared sacrifice in payment by business, government, individual households, and even, in some cases, payment by special groups like smokers, doctors, and hospitals.

The new compromise is forged from a belief that health care is both a right and an obligation: You have a right to expect access to health care but you have an obligation to pay your share of the tab. The compromise is a form of what I have called strategic incrementalism (incrementalism is going from one bad idea to another bad idea; strategic incrementalism takes steady steps toward a broader vision). The new compromise builds on existing public and private health insurance programs, it lets you keep what you have if you like it, it requires you to pay something for coverage if you have none, and it limits the behavior of health insurers in the marketplace.

The Massachusetts plan, Schwarzenegger's California proposal, and the plans of all the Democratic presidential candidates are close variants of this new compromise. Republican candidates as of this writing (in the early stages of the 2008 election) have shown little interest in embracing universal coverage through shared sacrifice, preferring instead a combination of tax credits and deregulation of insurance markets to stimulate competition. Still, while none of them has embraced the new compromise (or said much about health care in his campaigning), whoever emerges as the candidate on the Republican side will be forced to talk about health care as the general election heats up. Why? Because, after the economy, health care is the dominant domestic issue for Democrats and Independents, which is in sharp contrast to the Republican ranking of health care as an issue (behind the economy, immigration, and taxes).

A Real Debate

You could argue that the stars seem aligned for a victory for health reform, based on the new compromise, that leads to universal coverage, first in some landmark states like Massachusetts and California and then perhaps emulated through national policy. (I have always argued that Americans will not buy a car they haven't driven. So they will want to see the new compromise working before they sign off on it.) But it is plausible to expect a real debate about health reform that may actually lead to political change and in turn to legislation.

However, there are a few things to watch for:

God is in the details. While the new compromise has been embraced by politicians on either side, there can be large and important differences in the details such as which groups of newly covered are added at what rate and to what maximum level. Is universal coverage the goal, or is it simply significant coverage expansion ("universal coverage for some" was how an old colleague put it)? Similarly, while there is unanimity among Democrats about rolling back tax cuts for the rich to pay for health reform (and other things), unsurprisingly this view is not held by Republicans. Perhaps the most meaningful detail over which there is disagreement is in the degree of regulation or deregulation of the health insurance industry. Democrats are much more likely to tighten the rules on issuance, underwriting, and availability and funding of public versus private choices.

Political victory does not always mean legislation. It is one thing to speechify, to campaign, and to win an election with health care reform as a plank in your platform. It is quite another to get laws passed and enacted that make massive change in one-sixth of the U.S. economy. Every lobbyist and their dog is itching to get into the middle of this next round of change making.

Affordability. Here is my big concern. We may succeed in getting everyone an insurance card, but to reach that laudable goal we may be ignoring the need to transform a delivery system to make it better, faster, and cheaper than the system we have now. Giving people a card doesn't solve the fundamental cost problem, and there seems little in the candidates' proposals that will do much about the cost problem. We will have more people covered, and we will pay significantly more to achieve it. Without adequate cost controls we may be digging our children an even bigger fiscal black hole than the one they are already facing.

Health reform should happen—it could happen. But if it addresses only coverage expansion and ignores the issues of affordability, quality, and sustainability, we will have missed an opportunity to transform health care to deliver much higher performance for decades to come.

Meltdown

It's the stupid economy.

Author's note: *This essay was written toward the end of 2008, just as the U.S. economy was plunging into the abyss.*

The recent market meltdown is fundamentally reshaping the planet. As I write this, the Dow is bumping along at 8,500; world markets are shaken; and American families have lost trillions in net worth as home values tumble, as retirement accounts plunge (wiping out all the gains of the last decade), and as unemployment and job insecurity rise. Yet, health care seems like a safe haven to some of the investment pundits. In my view, health care will not remain unscathed by the economic collapse. Here are a few observations on the long-term effects of the recent market meltdown.

Reduction in the ability to pay. The current economic crisis is being felt by business, government, and households alike, severely constraining their ability to pay for health care. The payers' ability to pay is constrained in any recession, but in an environment of high government deficits, high household debt, shrinking corporate profits, and tight credit markets, the problems with ability to pay are aggravated considerably.

Pitting out-of-pocket health care costs against other household budget items. As recessionary pressures build and consumer purchasing power gets eroded, the rising co-pays and deductibles that patients face become even more onerous, leading to patients forgoing treatment and visits. Anecdotal evidence shows slowing consumer demand for prescription drugs, routine office visits, and elective procedures.

Searching for the value menu. In an economic slowdown we move to the value menu at McDonald's, but in health care we have few such options. With the exception of Wal-Mart's $4 generics and the retail clinics' very limited scope of service at affordable prices, there are not that many value choices in health care. Patients simply don't get the care, or they cut their medications in half or postpone the checkup or the procedure.

Supplier-induced demand. At the same time as consumers cut back, providers need to make up the shortfall. The classic health economics view of supplier-induced demand might rear its ugly head as providers try to promote more activity among the better insured and more affluent patients. Revenue cycle enhancement can become a cover for up-coding as well as for unnecessary tests and procedures for the affluent.

Rising number of uninsured and underinsured. Unemployment and rising unaffordability of care raise the number of uninsured, and those employers who want to provide health benefits often stay in the game by increasing cost sharing. As the number of uninsured and underinsured swell, providers will face increased costs of uncompensated care.

Rising cost of capital and credit. Health care is a huge employer and has a big payroll to meet. At the same time, hospitals and many other providers have enormous capital budgets for new construction, expensive new clinical technology, and electronic health records. The market meltdown is causing dramatic short-term spikes in the cost of credit, which foreshadow a longer-term challenge with the rising costs of capital.

The steep rise in short-term borrowing and the potentially tougher and more expensive capital lending requirements of the future could put a severe damper on the hospital construction boom, the rollout of electronic health records, and the pace of medical technology deployment. If operating income severely declines because of reduction in consumer demand and growing uncompensated care, the capital crunch will only worsen.

The NASDAQ dependent. I have always believed that American hospitals fall into three financial buckets. A third are doing just fine financially because of a favorable payer mix (which is code for "we don't see a lot of poor people") and sound management. At the other extreme, a third of hospitals are basket cases with unfavorable mix and/or poor management. In the middle are what I call the "NASDAQ dependent": They can't make money on patient care and they rely on investment income to balance the books. The NASDAQ dependent are being hit hard financially by this economic downturn even if patient volume remains strong.

Kaiser, too. It is not only hospitals that have a large dependence on investment income. In the most recently reported quarter, Kaiser made $400 million on health care but lost $700 million in investment income for a net $300 million overall loss. It could happen to any organization with big portfolios that support ongoing operations.

Bringing Medicare trust fund insolvency closer. The Medicare trust fund is projected to reach insolvency by 2017. Some have speculated that the economic meltdown will bring that forecast closer as budget projections shift.

The enormous Medicare unfunded liability of $35 trillion did not get much attention from the presidential candidates in the run-up to the election, primarily because any possible response would have involved painful and unpopular prescriptions, such as benefit cuts, payroll tax increases, raises in eligibility age, or clinical rationing—none of which has a feel-good ring to it. But if the economic meltdown brings the trust insolvency closer, it will inevitably grab the attention of the new president and Congress.

Retirement . . . forget it. I wrote long ago that the Baby Boomers will eventually have an epiphany and discover that they can never afford to retire, ever, largely because of the out-of-pocket costs of post-retirement health benefits. We are all going to be limo drivers in Boca Raton, working forever to pay the bills.

The recent meltdown underscores and turbo-charges the precarious position of retiree health benefits. Benefit consultants say we need $250,000 or more at retirement to pay for our expected lifetime out-of-pocket medical costs. Those lucky enough to have healthy 401(k) plans saw that amount evaporate from their retirement accounts in a matter of days in October. Boomers will be forced to work longer, and they will want to work for employers willing and able to provide health benefits until Medicare eligibility and beyond. Good luck to us all.

Effects of recession on government (particularly state and local government). Recession typically hits hardest at state budget coffers. With limited ability to run deficits, states face the double whammy of increased Medicaid and welfare rolls as revenues decline. Since states' finances typically lag behind a broader recovery, the budget hole could be deep and long, putting huge pressure on state and local government–funded safety nets for years to come.

Effect of the bailout on future spending. The federal government bailout, the wars in Iraq and Afghanistan, and the huge number of budget priorities at the federal level may have sucked all the available oxygen out of substantial health reform. The ability of the federal government to cover the growing ranks of uninsured will be limited by close to a trillion dollars tied up in economic recovery plans. No matter how popular or pressing, any large-scale health care reform proposals may have to be tailored to an austere time and may have to be phased in, postponed, or piecemealed to accommodate the economic realities.

However, the Obama administration may instead take the opportunity that the economic meltdown presents and make massive changes in the economy and in health care. It will all depend on whether the new president can sell—and the country can accept—massive short-term deficits in the name of long-run reform. Hey, we are in this for a trillion; what's another trillion?

I believe in the ability of Americans to respond to crisis, to change, to innovate, and to make money. While we are in a tough economic place right now, we should not bet against the American system. With smart leadership, sacrifice, and innovation, we might actually take this opportunity to build a sustainable future for the economy and for health care.

Obama's Re-election

Barack Obama doesn't have to do much
to ensure a second term—
just solve all the major problems.

Author's note: *This essay was written the day Obama was inaugurated as president.*

President Obama will be re-elected in 2012. All he has to do is restore faith in capitalism; reposition America in the world; reboot the American dream; rebuild our entire infrastructure; redirect the economy to sustainability; reverse global warming; resolve the Middle East, Iraq, and Afghanistan conflicts; remain steadfast in the defense of the American homeland; and reduce the trillion-dollar deficit. If he does that, he is a shoo-in for re-election in 2012. Oh yeah, there is health care. He needs to reform that, too.

The challenges are overwhelming, the starting slate of issues is daunting, and the expectations of his presidency are enormous. Yet, somehow the new president has to lead us through this mess and fix health care, too. Political analysts point to the fact that Obama must deliver on the promise to reform health care because the system is broken, and the voters who carried him to victory expect something big.

If he can help avoid a global depression, then the normal business cycle should kick in during his first term, so he may have progress to report on the economic front by 2012. The stimulus packages aimed at infrastructure and green technologies should make measurable progress by 2012 on climate change and infrastructure decay. Iraq seems to be winding down, although Afghanistan may be a thorn in the side of his presidency for a considerable time. And, though terrorists may test him early in his term, it is unlikely that Obama would respond alone, without support in the broader international community.

Health care may be harder. Not because there isn't a consensus that something needs to be done, but because there are so many competing interests in the $2 trillion industry. Policy analysts (myself included) are currently debating "big play" versus more incremental options available to the new administration. But if we take the longer view, what would constitute success for an Obama administration with regard to health care?

Real progress can be made, and if by 2012 the Obama administration can point to five big steps forward on health care, then reform will be deemed a big success.

Coverage Expansion

Without legislative changes, the number of uninsured will skyrocket early in Obama's term because of the economic meltdown. This will make coverage expansion a very steep uphill climb.

Universality may be even more elusive, but there is a growing belief that piecemeal solutions will unravel without a commitment to some broad endgame in which everyone has access to health care. The new administration can set the path toward universal care and make progress toward it, even through early incremental steps such as SCHIP [now the Children's Health Insurance Program] expansion and Medicaid support.

Affordability

President Obama and his advisers have pledged to make health care more affordable. But, as Stanford health economist Victor Fuchs and others have pointed out, there are a series of conundrums in the affordability debate. First of all, the voters define affordability not by how much health care costs as a share of GNP but how much they pay for it out of the household budget. (When health insurance is paid for mostly by their employers, most employees don't really feel they are paying for it out of their budget, but every economist will tell you they are.)

Comprehensive health insurance is unaffordable: A typical family policy with decent coverage can cost $15,000 per annum, an amount greater than the annual minimum wage in some states, and an amount that would swamp the household budgets of most families. The only way employers have found to reduce the cost of health insurance premiums is to jack up co-payments, deductibles, and premium sharing. We make health insurance more affordable to employers by making it less affordable to employees. So the first conundrum is that the tools to make health insurance premiums more affordable are the very tools that consumers and voters complain about.

The second conundrum is that health insurance is expensive because the delivery system is expensive. It is a convenient fiction that the greed of health insurers and/or pharmaceutical companies is at the root of expensive health care insurance. The truth is that the health care delivery system is expensive partly because of our collective greed: The providers of care, the consumers of care, and the suppliers of goods and services all want more.

- Consumers demand cutting-edge and often unnecessary or marginally expensive services and sue when we don't get them.
- Providers want higher incomes and tend to over-serve profitable procedures to attain those incomes.
- Suppliers of goods and services charge exorbitant prices for the same good received or service performed in different industries or different countries (everything from high-tech screws to software and accounting).

We tend to use overly expensive tools, in the hands of overly expensive people, with underwhelming and overly expensive results. The core of the conundrum is that everyone wants more affordable health care but they fail to see their part in the excessive cost.

The third conundrum is that the tools being proposed to reduce costs, such as health information technology, improved disease management and care coordination, and strengthening of primary care, while laudable, will require a major investment up front before any cost saving can be realized. And the evidence is weak that these tools will even reduce costs in the long run, either.

Affordability is the stated goal of the Obama administration, but these three policy conundrums need to be resolved before progress can be made. The key is in the next three benchmarks of success: delivery reform, payment reform, and administrative simplicity.

Delivery Reform

Advocates for organized systems of care will push hard for the Obama administration to favor integrated care systems in the policy process. Mayo, Kaiser, and other organized delivery systems will be looked at to provide leadership, but the real challenge will be for those providers in parts of the country with little history or experience in integration of care.

A key benchmark for delivery reform success will be whether the administration and Congress enact policies that can create meaningful delivery reform in all the disparate markets across America, not just in Minnesota and California.

Payment Reform

At the root of the transformation in the delivery system is a change in reimbursement to encourage high performance. There is near unanimity in wonkworld that payment reform is needed, and many agree on its shape. There is strong policy consensus to move toward episodic payment that rewards conservative, high-quality, coordinated care and away from "payment for procedures" in a fragmented delivery model.

Making this all work and turning it into both legislation and private market action may be the key challenge of the Obama administration's health policy. Without payment reform, delivery reform won't happen; without delivery reform, affordability will suffer; and without affordability, coverage expansion becomes more difficult.

Administrative Simplicity

Health care is mind-bogglingly complex, and there is real danger that all the necessary changes talked about here will make it even more complicated. Common-sense solutions that reduce complexity and can be communicated clearly will be hard to find, but they are badly needed. For example, building on existing and familiar administrative frameworks such as the Federal Employees Health Benefits Program may be easier to administer and sell politically than the creation of new and unfamiliar agencies and initiatives that add further layers of bureaucracy, both public and private.

President Obama has a lot on his plate. I wish him well. But if he can successfully address the issues on this list he will have earned re-election, and the opportunity to serve again in 2012 when the first of the Baby Boomers hit age sixty-five and become eligible for Medicare. If you thought your first term was challenging, Mr. President . . .

Disinformation, Division, and Delaying the Inevitable

How can there be a health care debate
when evidence doesn't matter?

Author's note: *This essay was written in the fall of 2009 as the health reform debate was building to an acrimonious conclusion.*

Oh, boy, did Obama get an earful this summer! Whipped up by Sarah Palin, Glenn Beck, and Rush Limbaugh, gun-toting seniors turned out in droves to protest Obama "death panels." "Get the government out of my Medicare" became the clarion cry (say what?).

It reminded me of my old one-liner: "I grew up in Glasgow, Scotland. In Glasgow, health care is a right, carrying a machine gun is a privilege. Maybe America got it the wrong way round." Weirdly prophetic.

The age of disinformation is upon us. Walter Cronkite is dead. Mainstream news anchors are competent, Teflon-plated vessels for synthesizing press releases. Newspapers and investigative journalists are a dying breed. Everybody with a computer or a cell phone has become a blogging, tweet freak. It is as if everyone in America has become a *New York Times* columnist, only without the brains or training.

And then came health reform. Against the backdrop of mainstream media in disarray, we are supposed to be having a civilized debate about health care reform, but it has turned into a national shouting match without any referees. An old mentor of mine used to say "there's no penalty for lying in the United States." Loony positions persist; ideas long discredited are given new life. Disinformation and lies are rampant. Despite valiant attempts by *The New York Times* and other credible news and public policy organizations to do fact-checking and "keeping them honest" comparisons, nobody believes the fact-checking stuff unless it confirms their biases.

The View from Each Corner

Making national policy in an ideologically divided country is tricky enough, but as media fragments and as we retreat into our Rush or Rachel corners, it is hard to see how the national shouting match becomes a national dialogue.

The Loony Right believes:

- All the uninsured are illegal aliens or extra-terrestrials.
- Paying doctors to discuss end-of-life care options with their patients is a death panel.
- Government can't run health care except for Medicare, Medicaid, the Veterans Health Administration, Tri-Care, the National Institutes of Health, the CDC, and so on.
- Incremental expansion of coverage on the existing employer-based health system is socialized medicine.
- Obamacare is evil.
- The French are even more evil.
- The British are evil and godless.

The Loony Left believes:

- If we can't have a single payer, we need a public plan, and . . .
- Public plans will automatically reduce costs without changing coverage or payment methods.
- Profits of insurance companies and drug companies account for all health care costs.
- The Congressional Budget Office is a front for United Healthcare's Ingenix division.
- Health industry lobbyists are running the government.

- Some people from Alaska are evil.
- The French are okay, but are turning evil because they are raising co-payments and deductibles to try and balance their budget.
- The British have free care paid by someone else (possibly the French).

As temperatures cool in the fall and deliberative bodies like the Senate Finance Committee finish their work, we may still have meaningful health reform that includes expansion of coverage, promising pilots on payment reform, and relief in the form of subsidies for many who have had no access to insurance coverage. But it is a small start on the path to transformation of health care delivery and payment.

Wanted: An Affordable System

The basic problem, as I try to emphasize over and over, is that the average American family cannot afford the average costs of health care. Affordable insurance can exist only if we have an affordable delivery system. There are not enough rich people to subsidize poor and middle-income people. We are living beyond our medical means, and it will sink our collective ship.

Health insurance is viewed as a magic source of money that can pay for all the care that anyone could possibly receive to prolong life or ameliorate disability, disease, discomfort, or disfigurement. But that endless source of money comes from all of us who pay premiums and taxes. And we cannot afford it.

If we cannot have a rational dialogue about a 3 percent increase in annual health care expenditure to cover the uninsured, how do we imagine we are going to deal with the more difficult questions of making health care cheaper than it is today, or how do we collectively consume less of it given an aging society and relentless scientific progress?

It is not going to be easy.

We are inevitably going to have to deal with the simple arithmetic of health care, namely: Health care costs equal the sum of health care incomes, which in turn equal the number of services we receive times the price of those services.

This means that we will have to have a long-run change in the delivery system that:

- emphasizes primary care and prevention over procedural interventions;
- expands the supply of primary care resources while restricting the supply and utilization of expensive and marginally effective high-technology interventions;
- emphasizes palliative care solutions instead of expensive futile care at the end of life;
- creates environments that encourage healthier behaviors and greater personal responsibility for managing personal health;
- simplifies the administrative mess by standardizing payment, measurement, and review systems;
- encourages medical technology innovators to produce new technology that is better, faster, and cheaper, not more expensive and worse; and
- encourages competition based on the creation of risk-adjusted outcomes for whole populations and individual patients rather than paying for procedures based on provider preference.

I would call it the "Bring Back Managed Care and Regional Health Planning in a Competitive Consumer-Directed Framework That Pays for Outcomes Not Procedures so We Can Ration Care Effectively and Fairly for All Americans Plan."

Catchy, eh? Do you think I should run for office? Or become French?

On structural change

The Myth of the Electronic Medical Record

We need to harness the positive energy
surrounding the electronic medical record
but curb our enthusiasm for it at the same time.

Don't get me wrong; I believe in the electronic medical record (EMR). I wrote an essay some time back arguing that the time had come when the environment, technology, and strategic commitment of key actors had reached a point where health care needed to start investing in information technology and making a difference in the way care is delivered. I still believe that, and reading fellow futurist Jeff Goldsmith's book *Digital Medicine* (Health Administration Press, 2003)—a must-read, by the way—reinforced the potential for IT implementation generally, and the EMR in particular.

So why the negative title for this essay? Here are three things that concern me.

Unrealistic Expectations

I have long argued that the EMR is a permanently emerging technology. It has been the future for the last thirty years and will be the future for the next thirty years. Recently, the EMR has received serious attention with the passage of the Economic Stimulus Act, but I fear that the expectations for it have risen alarmingly high at the policy, strategy, and practical level.

The EMR mavens of the left and right in Washington violently agree that a digital future will save lives, save money, and make us all happy. I hope this is true, but I suspect they are betting too much on what the technology can deliver, at least in the short run. More experienced hands are questioning the true payoff of an EMR even though they are making the investments. As one seasoned hospital CEO put it to me recently, "I am spending $60 million on the EMR. When all is said and done, I will improve quality but I won't save money. It will cost more."

The EMR needs to be implemented to improve safety, provide a better operating platform for the future, and help create a digital culture for the organization, but it is not the panacea that some in Washington might think.

The Power of Registries

In a whole series of meetings I have had over the years, from Canada to the Carolinas, I have become acutely aware of the power of simple disease registries, particularly for diabetic patients. Since by most estimates 70 percent of health care costs are for chronic diseases, one would think that we would all be focused on managing these patients. Unfortunately, neither the structure of the delivery system nor the reimbursement system nor the all-singing, all-dancing, hospital-based EMR does much to support the management of chronically ill patients.

What seems to work well is a simple registry of patients, with a system of clinical follow-up. I have heard people talk about how they have accomplished this effectively with sophisticated digital registries, but I also have heard from people who did it on an Excel spreadsheet, or 3-by-5 cards, or even graph paper (seriously), and realize almost the same results. The key is to follow up on patients and engage them in their own care. We need to learn this lesson: You don't need to spend $60 million to make a positive difference in health care delivery using information technology.

Stick to It

The hardest challenge of all is to stick to the task of implementation. As Kaiser has so ably demonstrated, vision and financial commitment to implementing electronic medical records have to be sustained over a long period of setbacks and false starts. Kaiser succeeded, after decades of effort, in its multibillion-dollar investment in a standardized EMR, and it is now reaping the rewards.

They have shown us the way. Now we must follow.

Time Out

*We need to put a halt to all the new technologies,
political prattle, and process improvement plans
and start anew with health care.*

Everywhere I go in health care as a patient, a family member of a
patient, or a futurist, I see that people in health care are really busy.
Actually, *frenetic* is a better term. Doctors are frantically pedaling
to keep up with medical innovation; declining reimbursement; and
waiting rooms full of patients who get older, fatter, crankier, and
more demanding every day. This is the hamster care I have described
elsewhere: Doctors are like hamsters on a treadmill of discounted fee
for service, scurrying faster and faster to make their target income as
real reimbursement per unit of service declines.

But nurses and other caregivers are even more harried. They live
in a world of hyper-documentation, of HIPAA compliance, of measurement of everything, of endless meetings and exhortations for
performance improvement, all enabled by information systems that
are feeble, disconnected, or nonexistent.

Health care delivery is like Jet Blue on a bad day, trying hard to
be cheery when it is overwhelmed.

High-Tech Chaos

As my wife was being cared for in a prestigious teaching hospital
with Magnet status, fabulous doctors and nurses, and shiny new
buildings, I watched the nurses scribbling on Post-it® Notes that they

placed on top of the keyboards of expensive mobile workstations that seemed to be permanently disabled. There were signs about infection control processes, warnings about name duplication of patients, and exhortations to wash hands everywhere you looked—a disorienting blizzard of quality improvement information.

My wife was surrounded by, and plugged into, an assortment of expensive-looking machines that we Americans love so much. "Machines that go ping," Monty Python once called them. No one seemed to pay much attention to them or the alarms that went off. The very expensive bed moved itself periodically, whether you wanted it to or not, making it virtually impossible for the patient to get comfortable.

Every few hours a whole new cast of characters became my wife's caregivers. Everyone did a great job, but I was struck that no one in their right mind would actually design work processes that way. Health care delivery really is *Pimp My Ride* writ large, with layers of gadgets and technological excess on a tired, old, and beaten-up chassis.

As a nation we experienced shock and awe that our brave military folk who have been wounded in Iraq were not receiving seamlessly coordinated care, that health care information systems for veterans don't talk to one another, and that there are significant failures in integrating sophisticated acute care with the rehabilitation and management of chronic conditions and serious mental illness so epidemic in Iraq veterans. But that's no different from the rest of us.

A Stop to the Madness

I do not blame the valiant doctors and nurses who are trying their best. I think they are overwhelmed. So I am proposing a mammoth time-out for health care. Here is how it would work:

Declare a technology moratorium. No new drugs or devices would be approved for two years until we learn how to properly use the ones we have. I suggest we pay the manufacturers exactly what we are paying them right now, but instead of selling new stuff, they send all their smart people into the hospitals and doctors' offices to apply their sophisticated business acumen in redesigning care processes so that they are efficient and effective. The technology vendors could still do R&D on new products, but the rules would be different when the moratorium ends: We won't buy anything unless it is better, faster, and cheaper than existing methods, otherwise it's not happening.

Ban the consultants. Futurists and health care consultants would be banished for two years unless they were prepared to do bedside management engineering, helping doctors and nurses design care processes that really work. There would be no conferences about the future of health care, PowerPoint presentations would be outlawed, and there would be no national meetings, unless they were authorized by the Institute for Healthcare Improvement.

Freeze the insurers. All insurers would be required to keep all the members they currently have. There would be no marketing or dropping of coverage, and all the money saved from their marketing budget would be sent to the Time-Out Czar, who would use the money to build a new delivery system from scratch for the uninsured.

Shut up the politicians. Politicians would not be allowed to talk any more about health care reform unless they specified how it was going to be made more affordable for the nation as a whole. Promising Magic Kingdom entry passes to a dysfunctional health care delivery system would be banned.

Furlough the doctors. All doctors would be furloughed at a salary of $500,000 a year for a specialist and $200,000 a year for a primary care doctor. They would be called back to staff a redesigned delivery system as needed. This suggestion actually might save a lot of money, because physicians' net income is only about 10 percent of health care costs. It is the economic havoc they wreak trying to get that income in a fee-for-service system that causes all the problems.

Zero-base the delivery system. Starting with the uninsured, the Time-Out Czar would design a rational delivery system. I started my health care career doing zero-based budgeting in Canadian health care. It was made fashionable in the late 1970s by Jimmy Carter, but the premise was simple: What would you do with your first dollar of expenditure, then with the next layer of spending, and so on, all to reach the optimum outcome?

At a meeting of emerging global health care leaders from Africa, Asia, North America, and Europe, I suggested that if you took the zero-based approach to health globally, you would start with spending your first health care dollar on clean water and condoms, then add lady health workers (as they do in Pakistan, where local women, not nurses, are empowered to give basic prenatal care, dramatically reducing infant mortality), then add immunization and hydration therapy for infants, then capitated primary care (as they do in Chile), then free generic drugs (as in South Africa), then basic outpatient surgical services. All of this could be done for probably less than $1,000 per capita, even in the United States. You would have to spend much more before you ever built hospitals or bought MRIs, but even developing countries fall into the trap of building fancy Western hospitals as a symbol of a great health care system.

Obviously, this is not a serious proposal. But if we do not pause and reflect on how to redesign the delivery of care; if we do not start to set priorities based on cost-effectiveness criteria; if we do not change the reimbursement system for providers to reward outcomes, not volume of marginally effective services; if we do not become more judicious in our introduction of new technology, we will bankrupt ourselves.

The Doctor Conundrum

*Why physicians are so unhappy,
and what we can do about it.*

Health care in America is a $2 trillion–plus, high-growth industry. Doctors are in short supply just about anywhere you go in the country. Many, if not most, family practice doctors are not accepting new patients. Even upper-class, well-insured patients have to wait a couple of weeks or more for a regular appointment with a specialist.

Doctors seem to be busy. Indeed, the surveys show that they are spending as much or more time on patient care activities than they did ten years ago—and the volume of procedures per physician is way up.

The stock of new physicians (new graduates minus retirees) is growing no faster than the population, but health care costs have been consistently growing at 6 percent to 10 percent per annum over the last decade or more. We are also smartening up as a nation and starting to reward physicians for quality improvement through pay-for-performance schemes.

Here are two more big factors: First, given that Baby Boomers have started to hit the early stages of total body breakdown, the demand for almost every medical specialty is poised to explode. And second, health reform will give insurance cards to 32 million people, and they may actually turn up for care.

Reasons to Be Cranky

It would seem to be a brilliant time to be a doctor. You have market power, a demographic and policy bonanza, lots of new technology to use that liberates you from the clutches of hospitals, patients who want to spend time with you, and an American society that appears to grant health care an ever expanding share of the economy. What's not to like?

How, then, can you explain the fact that in Harris Interactive/ Harvard surveys of physicians conducted for Strategic Health Perspectives, my colleagues found physician satisfaction at its lowest ebb since we started measuring it in the early 1990s? A full 43 percent are saying they are dissatisfied with their practice. Are these people nuts?

Well, I don't think they are crazy. Physicians are frustrated by administrative complexity, both public and private. They are angry at the constant threat of Medicare price cuts and the ongoing brinksmanship of negotiations over the sustainable growth rate. They feel they are losing autonomy to faceless bureaucrats in Washington; the state capitals; and Hartford, Connecticut. They see their patients as having to jump through mindless financial hoops that impair their compliance. They are happy about expanding science and knowledge and want to deliver good care, but the economic and administrative circumstances overwhelm the positives and put them in a black mood. Doctors are just cranky.

But what really pisses them off is the gap between their incomes and those of the rest of the high-end college graduates of America. The Center for Health Systems Change analysis of average physician income adjusted for inflation between 1995 and 2003 showed that income for all physicians declined by 7.1 percent over the period; for primary care doctors, by 10.2 percent; for medical specialists, by 2.1 percent; and for surgical specialists, by 8.2 percent. This is in sharp contrast to the 6.9 percent gain that all professional and technical workers made in the same period.

Put in stark local terms, my surgeon neighbors at Stanford drive Chryslers, my software neighbors drive Mercedes, my lawyer neighbors drive multiple BMWs (they are good at multitasking), and my venture capitalist neighbors have off-site garages to store their many exotic cars. If I were a doctor, the smartest kid in my high school class, the top 2 percent of my college class, and magna cum laude at Stanford, I would be pissed off, too. It is pretty bad when the lazy geography graduates like me make more than the surgeons.

Compensation Discrimination

While many like to point to the fact that doctors make more money in America than in any other country—which is true—they miss the big point. There are way more undeserving, highly compensated pigs at the health care trough than doctors.

Let's start at home. Consultants and futurists are paid four to five times what they would be in other countries; hospital CEOs, three to four times; administrators of all types, two to three times; and so on. CEOs of health plans who rack up $100 million plus in compensation over the course of a career are well ahead of the cumulative earnings of all the ministers of health in the developed world.

And then there are the salesmen and -women of America. I want my son to be a salesman because America rewards sales more than almost any other profession. There are armies of sales people in American health care, many of whom are making much higher incomes than the doctors they are calling on. These are just estimates; I urge someone with access to all these numbers (such as the compensation consultants) to publish them. Just wait and see how angry the doctors will be then.

The solution is not just to pay doctors more through fee-for-service upgrades or to tweak their incentives through petty pay-for-performance schemes. We need to imagine reimbursement systems that reward clinical excellence and professionalism and that provide incentives to do the right thing for patients, at the right time, in the right place, and by the right people (which may mean less expensive and more reliable auxiliary health professionals). We also need to look long and hard at whether we are rewarding acts of commercialism in health care more than the health care services that patients and society really want.

Clinical Reengineering

Progress can be made,
one care process at a time.

It's easy to get overwhelmed by the health care problem. At the system level, we struggle to cover all Americans, but we are daunted by the costs of system expansion, concerned about uneven quality and safety, and challenged by a shortage of trained professionals. It's easy to become depressed. Yet there is cause for hope. Across the country, individuals, organizations, and institutions are stepping up to make change happen at the grassroots level—one clinical care process at a time.

Historically, health care has paid inadequate attention to the language and practice of reengineering. In the late 1980s and early 1990s, every major industry in America embarked on a journey (which continues to this day) to improve quality and reduce costs. These industries paid systematic attention to business processes, information technology that rationalizes and streamlines those processes, and process improvement. All of this in the name of serving the customer, and making it happen better, faster, cheaper.

Health care is perhaps twenty years behind most industries on this journey. Admittedly, health care is complex, deals with matters of life and death, and has unusual organizational characteristics (such as the fact that some of the most important decision makers don't work for the organization). Yet we can't excuse ourselves in health care from the need to reengineer.

The good news is that we are recognizing the problem, we have advocates and experts who are gaining momentum, and there are success stories on the ground.

Recognizing the Problem

Clinical care is becoming more complex. Patients get older, fatter, and crankier every year. The majority of Medicare patients (some 55 percent) have five or more chronic conditions, leading one group of medical residents in the Carolinas to dub the typical patient as HONDAS (hypertensive, obese, noncompliant, diabetic, alcoholic, and/or all systems failing). The growth in numbers of multiple co-morbid patients puts additional strain on the system. It increases the complexity of intervention; adds to the challenge of lifting, transporting, and assisting patients; and heightens the stress nurses and other caregivers face in dealing with complex care regimens.

At the same time, we have an aging workforce and aging physical plants that were designed for a different era. The physical environment can impair efforts to improve care processes, and an increasing body of evidence from the Center for Health Design and elsewhere points to the fact that improved physical layout can have a positive impact on care processes and outcomes.

The rise of transparency has been a positive force in encouraging clinical improvement. But the downside is that the burden of measurement increasingly falls on caregivers at the bedside. Whether it is pay-for-performance systems, patient safety initiatives, outcomes measurement, or patient classification systems tied to mandatory staffing ratios, all of these put an additional data collection burden on frontline caregivers. Unfortunately, most electronic medical record systems, even when they exist, do not spontaneously capture all the required data for these new measures of clinical performance.

Trying to improve clinical care by simply throwing more resources at the problem does not seem to be a sustainable solution. (This is the micro version of "The Fallacy of Excellence" I wrote about on pages 55–57.)

Gaining Momentum

Path-breaking organizations such as the Institute for Healthcare Improvement (IHI) have long recognized the need to help health care transform at the clinical process level. Most recently through the 100,000 Lives Campaign and its sequel, the 5 Million Lives Campaign, IHI has rallied the field to improve in the name of patient safety and quality.

At the same time, we are seeing new evidence of how big the gap is between current practice and what might be possible in a better-designed care system. The ambitious time and motion study led by Ann Hendrich of Ascension Health and Marilyn Chow of Kaiser Permanente used multiple, sophisticated tracking tools to monitor the real behavior of nurses on typical med-surg floors. Their early results, and more yet to be published, found that nurses spend a relatively small part of their time (less than a third) in direct patient care. The rest of their time is spent in documentation tasks and "hunting and gathering" activities where they have to chase down equipment and supplies. These insights provide new evidence for the importance of redesigning clinical care processes to eliminate waste motion and to deliver improved patient care.

Keys to Success

As I travel around the country, I see growing interest in and commitment to clinical reengineering. Here are some observations about what's working well and why.

Importance of leadership. In almost every case of constructive change I have come across, leaders have placed an enormously high priority on clinical process improvement. Some leaders are leading this charge from a patient safety perspective, some from a quality and outcome perspective, and some more from a value perspective. But in all cases leaders are committed to redesigning care processes so they are safer and more reliable, they deliver higher quality care, and they eliminate unnecessary costs.

A willingness to look outside. Jeff Thompson, MD, CEO of Gundersen Lutheran Health System in Wisconsin, is committed to clinical redesign as a physician-CEO of a large and nationally acclaimed health system. Interestingly, he has hired system engineering experts from outside health care to work on the redesign. Similarly, Gary Kaplan, MD, another physician-CEO who is at Virginia Mason Medical Center in Seattle, is a believer in Lean Manufacturing. He has made regular site visits and undertaken immersion experiences in Japan's Lean Manufacturing culture, taking along his senior managers and board members to learn from outside health care.

Celebration of victory. While measurement may place a burden on frontline caregivers, it can also reward through demonstrable results. Most folk working in health care are genuinely committed to improving care, and most of them, particularly physicians, respond well to data-driven feedback. There is nothing more empowering than knowing you are doing a better job for patients every day.

Investing in clinical reengineers. Enlightened organizations are investing in specialized resources dedicated to improving care processes. For example, the Mayo Clinic has specialized staff designing new clinical processes in conjunction with frontline staff and creating working simulations of these process redesigns in specialized experimental space. But we need to take this idea much further and create armies of nurses, physicians, respiratory therapists, laboratory technologists, and other professionals who are cross-trained in systems disciplines. It is only when the frontline people are given the knowledge and skill to transform their work that we will have clinical processes that are effective and efficient for patients and caregivers alike.

Galapagos

*Health care species are perfectly evolved
for their environment.*

Charles Darwin turned 200 recently. By all accounts he nailed evolutionary biology the first time around in his *The Origin of Species*, showing how species evolve to survive in their unique environments. His work is still widely accepted (except for a few people here and there) as the blueprint for how evolution works. The core of his research stemmed from a visit to the Galapagos Islands, where he observed strange and unusual creatures, perfectly adapted to the unique environment in which they evolved. How would Darwin react to visiting American health care? He would surely feel his theory was vindicated, because health care is full of weird species perfectly evolved for a strange environment.

Here are a few examples of weird health care species that are thriving in their niche:

Catheterizers. Cardiac catheterization with balloon angioplasty is a procedure that saves a lot of lives, if done quickly after a heart attack, but there seems to be no benefit to a prophylactic balloon angioplasty done in patients who have no symptoms. Yet the catheterizers busily do these procedures all day long, even though they read the medical journals and go to the scientific meetings where all the evidence is laid out that the procedures they are doing don't make much sense. They keep doing the procedures because they can, they are in the cath lab anyway, it doesn't do much harm, and they get paid for it.

Revenue cycle managers. Armies of consultants optimize revenues for hospitals and other large providers. They scour for opportunities to code, capture, and charge more. By diligently pursuing every last dollar, they can justify their own fees and still boost the revenue of their clients. Doctors, too, find that the single best financial outcome from putting in an electronic medical record is increasing revenue capture. This is how we are going to use electronic health records to save money: by helping providers find more revenue. Say what?

By the way, the really smart consultants actually work for the providers and show them clever ways to increase revenue, and then they apply the same skills to helping the health plans (which pay the bill) find ways to minimize the newly inflated invoices they receive. This species is thriving.

Medicaid enrollment form fillers. About 150,000 of these creatures work in American health care. They fill out forms for prospective Medicaid enrollees and have a union-mandated productivity target of filling out two forms a day. To be fair, the forms are long and complex and require a lot of documentation. Until the recent market meltdown, it was easier to get a subprime mortgage than to get Medicaid.

Some would argue that the forms are long and complex to discourage people from applying, because if they apply successfully, then taxpayers have to pay for the Medicaid benefit. The strategy seems to be working: About a third of the uninsured in many states are people who are eligible for public programs but who, for a variety of reasons, don't apply. Yet we have a thriving number of people who administer the program and who are reluctant to embrace the automation that would make their jobs redundant. With the recent massive injections to Medicaid and the rising unemployment rolls, this species should do well.

Octuplet manufacturers. There is a small group of multiple embryo, in-vitro fertilizers who, despite professional guidelines and scientific evidence to the contrary, implant five, six, seven, eight embryos in "want to be" mothers, even when those mothers already have five, six, seven, or eight children. The most highly developed of this species do the IVF work on a private, cash-only, fee-for-service basis, and then send the impregnated mother back to Kaiser to have the babies and run up a large cost in the neonatal intensive care unit (NICU).

Repeat testers. This species replicates the work done by fellow species members. It all seems like wasted motion, but actually it works really well. Doctors order tests that have already been done by other doctors on the same patients because they don't know the tests were done, can't access the results, don't ask the patient, don't agree with the tests that were ordered, don't want to be sued for missing something, or are really eager for the ancillary revenue. This enables the species to thrive when their normal forage habitat (visit fees) is inadequate to meet income expectations.

Clinic closers. Some children's hospitals that have outpatient clinics with Medicaid reimbursement find it better to send patients to an affiliated, federally qualified community clinic. Instead of getting paltry Medicaid reimbursement, the federally qualified clinic gets a fee that is three or four or five times more than the Medicaid fee.

NICU runners. Prenatal care and normal deliveries are often not viable economically for hospitals. Many people in the baby business have to make it up on having a thriving neonatal intensive care unit that can bill a lot for very intensive care of low-birth-weight infants. Lack of investment in comprehensive prenatal care; rising numbers of births among teenage mothers, older mothers, and obese mothers; and impressive and expensive neonatal care techniques create continued demand for NICU services. Just make sure the NICU babies have some form of public or private insurance.

Large molecule makers. Pharmaceutical companies battered by generic substitution, growing cost sharing for brand-name drugs, and blockbusters coming off patent are all in pursuit of a new environmental niche called biologicals, or specialty pharmaceuticals developed through the tools of modern molecular biology rather than old-fashioned chemistry. Companies develop large-molecule drugs that are targeted at small populations and provide new therapeutic options for patients with previously untreatable diseases and symptoms, mostly cancer related.

Manufacturers have figured out a new pricing structure: They charge by the atom. Therapy for a year can cost tens of thousands if not hundreds of thousands of dollars. Because their drugs have large molecules, and they are promising improvements in treatment, they have set the price as high as the sky; no one wants to say no to improvements in care for dread diseases, no matter what the cost. Until now. The niche may be less viable as new policies encourage scientific studies comparing the comparative effectiveness of new technology with existing treatment, and as the Obama administration zeroes in on affordability of health care.

The combination of toxic incentives, Byzantine regulation, questionable ethics, lack of evidence, and organizational dysfunction creates a rich series of environmental niches in which weird species can thrive. No one would design creatures like this, but they have evolved to survive in their unique environment. Left alone, like the Galapagos, these creatures will continue to prosper, but as the health care environment changes, particularly the reimbursement system, then all these creatures will have to evolve to survive.

On lessons
from abroad

Aussie, Aussie, Aussie

Look "down under"
for health care solutions.

Well, it's health reform season again. Every ten years or so we get geared up to reform health care. We never actually do anything, but we have a great old time talking about it at conferences.

Periodically in health policy we ask if somebody else in the world is doing it right. Well, actually, every system around the world is an ugly compromise among cost, quality, access, and security of benefits, and almost all systems are in crisis according to the local news media. We in the United States have a bad bargain, maybe the worst: high costs, uneven quality, poor access, and no security of benefits except for those over age sixty-five.

Looking around the world, we find lots of things to learn from the United Kingdom, France, Germany, Canada, and others. One place that has my attention these days is Australia. I like Australia for the people, the wine, and the weather—and they swear a lot (which is really all I look for in a country). But Australia has a lot to teach us about health care, too.

Australia is a big country (bigger than the continental United States), but it has only 20 million people. Aussies are a no-nonsense, sarcastic, fun-loving, and friendly people who have a very low tolerance for pretentiousness—my kind of people. On one visit I had a chance to meet with the nation's top CEOs of health plans and learn a little about what Australia is doing. Australia can teach us some important lessons as we reform health care in the United States.

The Aussie Health Plan

All health care systems are difficult to describe, and all reflect the culture and values of the country. Here is a very brief and simplistic overview of Australia's health care system.

Imagine the Canadian system as a base (a national health system funded through taxes that provides all ambulatory care and has public hospitals where care is effectively free to residents, although their choice of specialists and amenities in the hospital would be somewhat limited). This is what Australians call Medicare.

Add to that a private insurance system that supports hospital care in private hospitals and in higher-amenity environments in public hospitals for people with private health insurance. The private system is not dissimilar to the United Kingdom's. The big difference is that, while less than 10 percent of Brits have private insurance, nearly 50 percent of Australians have some form of private coverage that was purchased directly by families and individuals. And unlike the United Kingdom, where the private sector has historically been characterized as queue jumping for minor procedures like varicose vein removal, the Australian private system covers about half or more of chemotherapy, joint replacement, and other high-tech care.

Private insurance in Australia is relatively cheap by our standards, mostly because it is supplementary insurance, with a cost (depending on the type of coverage purchased) from a few hundred dollars a year up to about $3,000 (Australian) for "Rolls Royce" coverage. Experiments are under way to fund health services through private insurance "outside the hospital gate," as they say Down Under, meaning in the ambulatory environment.

Overall, the nation spends about 10 percent of its GDP on health, compared with 16 percent in the United States. The people seem as happy as anyone else, based on international surveys, and they live longer and seemingly better than we do. I think it's the beer, the beaches, and the barbie that do it, not the health care, but that's another story.

Incentives

How do Australians manage to get people signed up for a two-tiered system and deliver what seems a pretty decent value to all Australians? Here are some clues that we might learn from:

An explicit choice/cost trade-off. Australians face a clear and seemingly socially acceptable choice: You can have free care, paid by you and your fellow taxpayers, but you will have no choice of provider for specialty hospital–based care, and you will not get the fancy private room unless you are devastatingly ill. Or you can buy a private insurance policy and have complete choice of provider, no waiting, and higher amenities. If you buy the private insurance (as in the United Kingdom), you still have to pay your taxes to the Australian Medicare system, and all Australians get pretty much the same primary care and ambulatory public services. Private patients care about the public system because they are subsidized by the public system while in the hospital, in that Medicare is paying for a significant portion of the private patient's stay. That is one reason the private insurance system accounts for only 11 percent of overall funding for health, despite its 50 percent penetration of the population. Overall, Australia is a very interesting example of what the Europeans call social solidarity, blended with and supplemented by private insurance. It will be interesting to see as the private sector grows outside the hospital gate whether the solidarity remains so solid, but to date, the Aussies seem to have broad buy-in for the system, with the exception perhaps of trade unions and the political left.

A simple tax subsidy. In the last decade, Australia has experimented with tax-based inducements for individuals to purchase insurance. It tried means-tested subsidies, but those did not seem to work, and Aussies have now hit on a 30 percent flat rebate as a way to stimulate growth in the private system. It seems to be working like a charm. Since the introduction in 1999 of the rebate and lifetime health coverage guarantees (I'll say more about the latter below), enrollment in private insurance, which was dwindling at around a third of the Australian population prior to the reform, jumped dramatically to almost exactly half of all Australians being covered by some form of private insurance (with 43 percent having coverage for hospital care). It's not just the richest half who signs up. A quarter of those with private insurance has annual household incomes of less than $33,000 Australian (about $27,000 in U.S. dollars), and half of all privately insured Australians have household incomes of less than $70,000 (Australian), which is about $58,000 U.S. and pretty close to the U.S. median household income. My impression from the Sydney news media and local ads for coverage is that buying health insurance is viewed as a no-brainer for the middle class, largely because of the tax subsidy.

Incentives to sign up young and stay in. Critics of private insurance point to the classic sources of market failure: cream skimming, adverse selection, and moral hazard. True, Australia has to be wary of all of these. But it has developed a sensible inducement to sign up when you are young and healthy and stay in for life. Most importantly, private health insurance in Australia is community rated, and a reinsurance pool handles the risk adjustment that could face insurers that get disproportionate enrollment from the elderly or the sick. (What a radical idea! I am still mystified that we in the United States abandoned community rating over the last twenty years with seemingly no public or political debate about the consequences of the shift.) In addition, as part of the 1999 reform, Australians thirty years old or under who sign up for private insurance pay a lower premium throughout their lifetime than those who postpone enrollment. People over the age of thirty will face a 2 percent increase in premium over the base rate for every year they postpone joining an insurance plan. Brilliant. (Recent legislative changes remove this penalty after people have paid the increased premiums for ten years because research showed that it was a reason people abandoned private health insurance. Again, this latest move is targeted to keep the younger people enrolled.)

The employer has no role. The Australian system is about government, private insurers, and consumers figuring out how to get along. Employers are out of the picture. There is almost no group insurance, and almost no employer sponsorship of health insurance. Who needs it if you have community rating and risk adjustment? Australian businessmen do not have to fret about how health care costs are eating their earnings per share. They just have to pay their taxes and let their employees figure out on their own if they like the value proposition of private health insurance.

Marketing and administration costs are low. The traditional rap against individual insurance markets is that they have astonishingly high administrative costs to pay brokers, do underwriting, and so forth. It appears that this is not the case in Australia. Total administrative costs of private insurance (including profit) are around 9.5 percent, way less than in the United States. This is partly because the products seem to sell themselves as a result of the tax subsidy, partly because they are simple and not overly expensive products, and partly because the industry is efficient and seems to operate in a form of collegial competition through regional oligopolies rather than through an advertising and marketing arms race.

Containing costs through the pharmacy benefit scheme. The private-sector CEOs of health plans in Australia love the nation's pharmacy benefit scheme, a universal system of coverage paid by the Commonwealth (the federal government), which covers most medications through a very tight, price-controlled, reference-price-based system. It is a system that is detested by every global drug company but is enthusiastically embraced by the health plans (or health funds, as the Aussies call them).

Where Do They Go from Here?

I gave a little talk in Sydney to a group of health fund leaders about what we are doing in America about value purchasing, transparency, pay-for-performance, and so on, and the Aussies seem interested in embarking on many of these initiatives. Indeed, my mate Dr. Michael Armitage, a former health minister of South Australia and current CEO of the Australian Health Insurance Association, is pursuing many of these initiatives with his members. In other areas, like health IT, the Aussies are way ahead of us.

There is no such thing as a perfect health care system. But Australia has wrestled, I think successfully, with big issues such as the balance between public and private coverage, the role of employers, the value of tax subsidy, simplicity of insurance product design, and coordination of public and private controls for new technology. Australia is worth a visit for a whole host of reasons, including some ideas about health care. So as the Australian tourist board ad says: "Where the bloody hell are you?"

French Lessons

*How to have the best health
and health care in the world.*

The French have the best health care system in the world. Just ask them. (According to them, they have the best everything in the world, from cheese to lifestyle.) Yet, the World Health Organization and many international comparative analyses actually do agree that the French are healthy and that the French health system is at, or close to, the top of the list in performance. Are there any lessons that we can learn from France?

Decoding French Culture

All health care systems are a reflection of the values and culture of their country. So you can decode the health care system only if you try to understand the culture. On a recent visit, I did my best to immerse myself in the language and culture to interpret why the French seem to be so healthy and do so well in the health care comparison stakes. This involved a lot of wine and smelly cheese.

Here are some clues:

The country is in a superior location. France is geographically situated as a perfect hexagon (*L'Hexagon,* they call it) in the temperate zone of the northern hemisphere, which gives the country beautiful vistas, rich arable land, and the finest products of the countryside. From the cheese of Normandy to the olives of Provence and all the wine in between, France has killer natural groceries. Even the poorest peasant (read: "guy who just sold his little farm to some chinless Brit hedge fund manager") knows what good organic food is (they call it *biologique*).

The chain supermarkets (the equivalent of Safeway) are filled with dead chickens with their heads still on. If you ask for ground beef (don't ask for hamburger; they will know you are American), they actually take a piece of beef and grind it up in front of you. In most American supermarkets, a pound of ground beef could conceivably be sourced from many different cows, in many different countries. So they eat better in France. While we subsidize big agro-business to make high-fructose corn syrup (the true weapon of mass destruction in our society), the French subsidize little farmers to grow chickens with their heads still on and to make an enormous variety of smelly cheese.

They have superior education. France has an incredibly merito-cratic education system in which the top of the class moves up the educational hierarchy so that if you make it to the top you really are the smartest in France. Since the French are the smartest people in the world (in their assessment) and their system is meritocratic, by definition anything that these smart people decide has to be the right thing to do. Very Descartes.

The French are smarter than the market. (Or so they think.) You see this everywhere in France: A spectacularly engineered, uniquely French solution is carefully crafted to deliver superior performance, but it is weird, idiosyncratic, and completely lacking in export potential. Renault Espace minivans can be driven for hundreds of miles at fantastic speed on a single tank of diesel, but I defy you to operate the parking brake. They don't sell in America.

They have a superior lifestyle. The French believe their country and their lifestyle are superior, and it seems that much of the French economy is focused on lifestyle maintenance. This ranges from the billions of euros spent polishing French roads and villages, to the parades of guys in Paris who are dedicated to cleaning the streets and ridding the sidewalks of *merde du chien*.

My personal favorite lifestyle maintenance policies are the com-bination of regulation and subsidies that exist to maintain French eating habits. For example, in every Paris neighborhood there has to be at least one *boulangerie* open to sell fresh bread every day (this means a bakery can close Sunday or Monday but not both, and bakeries have to coordinate this with their geographic competitors). The price of a baguette is set by law!

Similarly, the French have a system of lunch money subsidy in which employers can give lunch coupons to employees that are tax deductible so that an employee can afford to go to some brasserie for *moules frites* and a carafe of wine for an hour and a half, every workday. The goal is to keep the brasseries open and not let McDonald's get the business. But let's face it, if you had a *moules frites* subsidy and a mandatory thirty-five-hour workweek, you'd live a long, healthy life, too.

They drink wine in moderation. French kids learn to drink wine at an early age, usually watered down. Decent *vin du pays* is cheaper than Coca-Cola in most restaurants and supermarkets. The French (like most Europeans) learn how to drink before they learn how to drive. In America, we unleash fifteen-year-olds on to the streets in SUVs so they can drive to Safeway with their fake IDs, but they can't have a glass of wine with a meal until they are twenty-one. No wonder we have an entire generation of college graduates who are not sure what happened in college because of Jäger bombs.

No stress: They don't sweat the big stuff. In the early 1990s a colleague and I were giving a briefing in Paris to a big fancy French company explaining how because of globalization, the American wave of reengineering would eventually hit France and require tough choices, a dedication to efficiency, and streamlining of business processes. An incredulous French executive barked back at me: "Why would we do that? It will ruin our life!" He had a point. While we in the United States have driven ourselves into a frantic BlackBerry orgy of overwork over the last two decades, the French are still pretty chill.

They do sweat the small stuff. The French do worry like crazy, but not about big things like war, their job, fidelity, and so forth; they obsess over the small stuff. Every French movie has a scene where a bunch of people are sitting around eating in someone's kitchen and the dialogue goes something like this:

"The peaches are not so fresh today, Jean Claude."

"You are right, the peaches we had yesterday were much fresher, but they came from Auvergne. These peaches did not come from Auvergne, you know . . ."

This conversation goes on for another fifteen minutes, and American audiences watching the movie have dozed off reading the subtitles, their popcorn strewn across the floor. But the French love worrying about this kind of stuff; it is like therapy for them.

They walk. Parisians walk. Take the Metro. Walk. When Madame goes to the village for the second time that day, for another fresh baguette for the evening meal, she walks. My wife noticed that all the under-thirty women in Paris are in sensible but stylish flat shoes, ready for long hours on the pavement. Even though aging French Dolly Birds are still sporting high-heeled boots for the winter, they are still walking in them.

They walk upstairs. The average American MRI is larger than the average Parisian elevator. While we in the United States are supersizing our MRIs and hospital beds (even to the point of installing ex–port authority cranes to get the patients out of bed), the French make the elevators so small and claustrophobic that overweight people like me are forced to take seven flights of stairs to the apartment. (This happened.) Voilà, we are thin.

They use public transit. From the Paris Metro to the spectacular TGV (high-speed train), French of all socioeconomic strata use public transport. The TGV hurtles through the beauty of the French countryside at 200 miles an hour, and you arrive relaxed. This sure beats hurtling through Trenton on Amtrak or schlepping through O'Hare. And when they get off the train? You guessed it: They walk.

They get naked in the summer. If you visit the beaches of St. Tropez in the summer, you will indeed encounter the topless Eurotrash tottering around on tiny heels, on the arm of the Russian mob oligarchs who now rule the South of France. But, mostly, you see naked middle-aged people. Way too much information. However, getting naked every summer in front of your Gallic peers is a powerful motivation to keep the BMI in check.

They smoke. Sure, they don't smoke as much as they used to, and smoking is now outlawed in restaurants, bars, and all public places, but you still see a lot of smokers, particularly young people, and they are thin. (This phenomenon is most pronounced in Croatia, where young people look like they came from the United States in the 1970s, a full 30 pounds smaller. It's like a time warp back into an episode of *Charlie's Angels*.)

They take drugs. The French are the highest consumers of pills in the world. The pills are cheap because the French tightly regulate pharmaceutical prices for most products unless they are truly innovative. (Some cynics might say that *innovative* means "made by French drug companies"; see "They have superior education," above.) The green crosses of French pharmacies are everywhere in France: from every block in Paris to every village in Provence. And pharmacists can prescribe many medications. France has lots of little special medications for the liver, and you will always see Monsieur popping a little pill or two after the cheese plate to aid the digestion.

They revere liberté, egalité, fraternité. The French like liberty as much as we do; indeed, they gave us a statue about it. But they are also big on equality and fraternity. The more contemporary term in Europe is *solidarity*, which is the recognition that certain key dimensions of society such as health care, education, and transportation are collective goods that need to be supported by all, for the benefit of all. Over the last decade or so in the United States, we talked a lot about liberty. Fraternity, not so much.

Alors, you got it. The French are different from us. We won't have the same health status as the French because our values and culture are different. We are a little too hard working, money obsessed, frantic, and unequal to have the French lifestyle. But what about the French health care system? Is there anything we can learn from them that is translatable, given the wide cultural differences?

A Translation for America

T.R. Reid's excellent book, *The Healing of America: A Global Quest for Better, Cheaper, and Fairer Health Care* (Penguin Press, 2009), is a wonderful review of how many other industrialized countries provide health care that is less expensive and fairer. From his work, here are a couple of ideas we should think about that don't actually require us to turn French.

Carte Vitale. The French have a ubiquitous electronic smart card called Carte Vitale that contains basic health information on the patient. It is really a portable electronic health record and insurance card. Doctors also swipe it through a card reader for billing purposes. There are no billing clerks in the doctors' offices because it is all *automatique*, as Reid's French doctor would say. It's all very French proprietary technology. The French are big on smart cards and little card readers that they design and manufacture, but the basic idea is right: Everyone should have a card he carries about that with one swipe conveys the essential patient information and links to his health insurer.

Normally in the United States we embody the intelligence in the network, not in the card, but given the billions being spent on health IT, surely to God we can have a system in which at least the doctor knows you are allergic to penicillin and the billing part is taken care of. I really want to see an end to the pathetic U.S. ritual that takes place in most doctors' offices: The receptionist takes your health insurance card and makes a copy of it, both front and back. In the age of Google this ritual is positively medieval.

Skin in the game and price transparency, French style. As Reid explains, the French require insurers by law to reimburse doctors and patients within a timely manner (usually within three days). But here's the good part: The French system expects patients to pay something at the point of care and, indeed, as Reid explains: "Most French patients in fact pay the full charge of treatment at the point of service." There is a detailed price list in every office; you, the patient, pay with your own money at the point of care; you know what the deductible and cost sharing will be, because the Carte Vitale knows; you put down your euros; you get the service; and what you are being reimbursed has to be paid to you by the insurer within three days.

Contrast this with the bizarre, gotcha, after-the-event surprise you get when encountering American health care. You don't know until it's over what you just bought and for how much. It's like the New Jersey freeways: The exit signs are after the exits.

So in conclusion, read T.R. Reid's book for more great insights on the French and other health systems. There are countless lessons on how to make health care fairer and cheaper that we could easily adopt for American consumption. And if you really want to be as healthy as the French: Walk, eat cheese, drink wine, throw away your BlackBerry, and get naked in the summer . . . but please don't smoke. As the French cigarette labels say, *Fumer Tue* (Smoking Kills).

Dr. T and the Canadian Medicine Show

*We can learn from Canada and other countries
about care, not just coverage.*

Health reform has largely been about expanding coverage to the previously uncovered and regulating unsavory health insurance practices. But we also have to make the health care delivery system work better, so it is of higher quality and is more affordable than today; otherwise we will bankrupt ourselves in the long run. We need good ideas from anywhere we can get them.

International comparisons, such as the wonderful surveys conducted by Harris Interactive for the Commonwealth Fund, illustrate the substantial and rapid progress that countries such as Australia, Holland, and the United Kingdom, in particular, have made in improving the performance of their health delivery systems and embracing many of the tenets of superior health care performance that most U.S. policy experts hold to be self-evident: ubiquitous use of electronic health records in primary care, pay-for-performance, chronic care disease registries, and so on.

But even in the face of such fresh and compelling evidence, most Americans quietly do the nudge, nudge, wink, wink thing and say to each other: "Well, Britain or Holland might be OK for routine primary care, if you like waiting rooms, but where would you or your loved ones want to go when you need complex, high-technology interventions such as pediatric craniofacial reconstructive plastic surgery? You would want your child in a fancy American hospital, not in Canada or Britain. Right?" Well, maybe not.

The Story of Dr. T

Dr. T is an Ivy League–trained, subspecialist reconstructive cranio-facial plastic surgeon who, after completing long years of training at the world's greatest academic institutions (you institutions know who you are—all 300 of you—so I will not name you, in order to honor Dr. T's request for anonymity), spent a year in Canada at a large, prestigious pediatric academic health center.

I was lucky enough to be introduced to Dr. T and, based on my interviews with her, I offer a few of her key observations from practicing her craft on both sides of the border:

Quality of nursing care. Dr. T stressed the amazing quality of nursing care in Canada, compared with that at the most prestigious hospitals where she had worked in the United States. As she put it: "Nurses in Canada seemed more dedicated, more professional, more specialized, more vested in the care of the patients, and more empowered than their American counterparts." She attributed the differences to leadership, specialization, preparedness, and continuous training of staff.

For example, when Dr. T conducted a complex reconstructive plastic surgery operation in Canada that took several hours, she never once had to ask for a specific instrument to be handed to her because the nurses knew, and had carefully documented, a workflow protocol for each surgeon that the chief OR nurse had developed. In contrast, in the prestigious U.S. academic medical center where Dr. T now practices, she had to spend hours orienting the team to the complex procedure they were about to conduct. In the American hospital, no dedicated RN scrubs for the case; instead, a floating surgical technician is assigned to that OR for that day. Like ships passing in the night.

Working at the tip of a very large referral pyramid. Dr. T is among the most specialized, highly trained, subspecialty surgeons on the planet. When she was practicing in Canada, she and her colleagues were referred virtually all the complex cases of their type in the region, if not the entire country. In Pennsylvania alone, there are four pediatric craniofacial plastic surgery centers, each competing for the same patients, and presumably operating with reduced volumes of truly specialized cases.

The benefits of a large, concentrated referral pyramid are that outcomes improve through specialization of skills. This is the classic volume-outcome effect. The surgeons, OR team, and nursing teams have dedicated staff that work on nothing but these complex cases.

In the United States, we have way too many facilities doing way too many complex cases, mixed in with the run-of-the-mill money-makers. American specialists are often "amateurs" in the sense that they practice their true subspecialty craft less than half the time. Because there are fewer specialists per capita and a nationwide health plan, Canadian referral hospitals can build large referral pyramids, create significant volumes, and organize dedicated high-performance teams to conduct complex procedures.

Administrative waste motion. When I talked to Dr. T, she was weary at the end of the day working in her American hospital—and not because she had just finished a long day in the OR. She was weary and frustrated because she had spent three hours after the case was done Googling for Current Procedural Technology codes to make sure she billed correctly for the complex multipart procedure she had conducted that morning.

Her anxiety was not about maximizing revenue for herself or her institution. (I'm sure the institution would prefer her to be anxious about revenue cycle management, as the CFOs call it.) No, she was anxious that she would "commit heinous fraud on the insurer for billing inappropriately." Although she spent seven years in surgical training, she admits she is a novice at coding, which can now dominate much of her time. What a complete waste of precious human capital.

Economic discrimination in clinical care. In Canada, if Dr. T received a patient referral, the first thing she would do is to figure out the best way to take care of the patient. She would never even give the patient's financial or insurance status a second thought because it is irrelevant to clinical decision making in most of Canadian health care.

On her return to practice in the United States, Dr. T has been unpleasantly surprised by her clinical colleagues who perform "economic triage of patients," in which specialists avoid taking cases because the insurance coverage is lacking. Dr. T spends two to three hours every day "fighting the system" (with insurers, her clinical colleagues, and hospital administrators) to secure the approval for services that her patients need, whether it be an operation or simple therapy.

Rogue warrior practitioners. In Canada, Dr. T felt she was part of a team with her physician colleagues, the nursing staff, and the hospital leaders. On her return to the United States, she feels more like a fellow combatant among the "rogue warrior physicians."

Pointless pluralism. Her Canadian hospital had a "clunky electronic health record," but at least it was standardized across the institution. (Canadians are behind even Americans in their pathetic deployment of EHRs). Her American hospital, though, has thirty different health record systems, with each specialty service organizing its own clinical charting systems, none of which talk to each other. "I cannot even share my notes with the doctors across the hall," she told me.

High performance in shabbier surroundings. When Dr. T went to Canada, she found the OR rooms and clinical corridors were a bit dingier, and she had to walk down the hall to access a shared printer. This is frustrating when you are trying to crank out research papers on top of a full clinical load. (I can relate to the printer part, at least. When I was a young health services researcher at the Vancouver General Hospital in Canada, I shared a subterranean, converted broom closet with two other colleagues. It was at the end of a former secure prison ward, converted to care for long-term geriatric patients. We had to drive 12 miles out to the university campus to access a computer, let alone a printer.)

The built environment of some Canadian hospitals may be a little shabbier than the Shanghai-like Crane Fest that is the American academic medical center. (Academic medical centers have been on a decade-long orgy of new construction analogous to the Chinese office building boom.) But don't assume marble atria lead to superior clinical performance. Dr. T is nostalgic for the shabbier, high-performing Canadian setting. And instead of just sitting back and accepting it, she has joined her hospital's quality improvement committee and will dedicate even more of her precious time and skill to making her hospital a better place for patients. She doesn't know whether to laugh or cry when she hears her educated colleagues insist we have the best health care system in the world.

Time to Lose the Ancient Anecdotes

Dr. T's experience represents, as far as I can tell, the closest thing to a real-time, double-blind trial of cross-border, comparative high-tech, superspecialty care. Most pundits who opine on the good or bad of other countries' systems are usually relying on ancient anecdotes about how their Aunt Betty in Winnipeg had to wait nine years for a hip replacement and that wouldn't happen in Wisconsin. Yawn, yawn.

I am as guilty of this as anyone. But at least Canadian health care for me is not some obscure policy abstraction: It is the system where my sister and all of my wife's family get their health care, and we have countless Canadian baby boom friends. All of our friends and family on both sides of the border are dealing with the same breast cancer, prostate cancer, knee replacement, hip replacement, heart attack, and chronic care issues on a cross-border basis. So I live with the stories and the realities of the good and the bad on both sides of the border.

As I have written before, all health care systems are an ugly compromise among cost, quality, and access. There is no perfect system. But what is pretty clear is that we in the United States get about the worst bargain compared with most developed countries.

Canadian health care remains an annoying comparison to American health care because it is so close:

All Canadians live in American media markets. Canadians are subject to all the Viagra ads on American TV channels, even though the ads are illegal in Canada.

Canadian doctors are equivalent to American doctors. They pass the same exams and have pretty similar training. Although Dr. T did point out to me that the Canadian system paid more attention to actually educating their medical residents and fellows than exploiting them as under-compensated service providers.

Canada now spends 7 percent of GNP less on health care than America does. Yes, you do have to wait a bit for a recreational MRI of the tennis elbow in Canada. But Canada could buy a lot of MRIs with 7 percentage points of GNP. At a 10 percent per annum lease rate, Canada could lease 84,000 MRIs with the difference, enough for every hockey team in the country. They wouldn't do it, of course, because they view it as a complete waste of money.

Canadians drive the same cars, eat the same cheeseburgers, and eat even more doughnuts than Americans.

Canadians are different in values, however. They describe themselves as unarmed Americans with health insurance.

Lessons for American Health Care Organizations

In closing, I asked Dr. T to use her cross-border experience to synthesize her advice for the American health care system. Here's what she told me:

Refuse to accept that medicine is a business like any other. For one, there is no other business where the customers don't know what they are getting and for how much. If treating medicine as a business worked best, then why should governments interfere? Yet most countries, including all those that score much better than we do, accept that the best care comes from some government oversight. If we give in to the notion that the market knows best, even in the absence of a true health care market, we lose the ability to prioritize what really matters to us as citizens and physicians.

Get the incentives right. Dr. T has seen salaried academic surgeons and fee-for-service surgeons, on both sides of the border, and she believes that some combination of salary and performance incentives tailored to the specialty is essential to enhance quality, productivity, and outcomes. I couldn't agree more.

Build high-volume regional referral pyramids. Dr. T believes that large, regional referral pyramids reduce costs and improve quality, with all the attendant benefits of specialization at the physician, nursing, and OR team level. As a former regional planner, I admit she had me at "hello."

Empower nurses. Dr. T believes nurses need to have a real stake in the organization and feel empowered that they are the central caregiver for the patient. In too many American hospitals, nurses are treated as just a cog in the wheel, or they diminish their own professional status by focusing on collective bargaining issues rather than on clinical leadership and professional development. I am married to a Canadian-turned-American former ER triage nurse-turned–nursing administrator who, when she first practiced in America, said to me: "Boy, do nurses ever kowtow to doctors down here." Enough said.

Fix the financial matters. Dr. T needs to be relieved of the administrative nuisance and financial rationing that is plaguing American medical practice. Much of it, as Dr. T points out, is self-inflicted pluralism. Doctors need to accept standards, compromise on choices of systems and tools of the trade, and participate actively and enthusiastically in the kind of heavy-duty clinical reengineering so effective at Mayo Clinic, Cleveland Clinic, and Kaiser Permanente, among others.

Be driven by outcomes . . . Canadian physicians in Dr. T's experience embraced evidence-based medicine far more than did her American colleagues. She was admonished after her first case in Canada for administering prophylactic antibiotics because it was not an evidence-based practice. As a consequence, patients with multiple resistance to antibiotics were rare in her Canadian hospital but ubiquitous in her American hospital.

. . . Not just by incomes. Tommy Douglas, the former Saskatchewan premier who was the father of the Canadian health care system, was recently voted as the Greatest Canadian Ever in a national poll in Canada, beating out in a landslide Wayne Gretzky, Bobby Orr, and some pretty decent figure skaters. Tommy's great quote was: "When people say, 'It's not the money, it's the principle' . . . it's the money."

Let's hope there are lots more young Dr. Ts out there for whom medicine is about bringing compassion to the care of the patient, not just worrying about the money.

On leading
and legislating

The Five Pillars
of Leadership

Health care at all levels,
from presidential policy to bedside decisions,
is overmanaged and underled.

Health care is complex. It is full of professions, guilds, unions, and community stakeholders, which make leadership difficult. How do you lead in such an environment?

1. *Distinguish between managing and leading.* This is at the heart of the health care leadership problem. Health care at all levels, from presidential policy to bedside decisions, is overmanaged and underled. What's the difference? You can do no better, in my view, than John Gardner's definition in his classic book *On Leadership* (Free Press, 1990). To paraphrase Gardner, leaders distinguish themselves from the general run of managers in at least six respects:
   - They think longer term.
   - They understand the relationship between their organization and the wider environment.
   - They reach and influence stakeholders beyond their own organization's boundaries.
   - They put heavy emphasis on the intangibles of vision, values, and motivation, and they understand intuitively the nonrational and unconscious elements in both leading and following.

- They have the political skill to cope with the conflicting requirements of multiple constituencies.
- They think in terms of renewal and adaptation to an ever changing reality, not just sticking to the system.

2. *Respect leadership as a political process.* Leading an organization is more like running a small country than managing a large store. Leadership is inherently political, which frustrates many promising managers who have been promoted because of high marks, good work performance, and self-righteous excellence. In a world of coalition building, compromise, and horse trading, these managers get frustrated, and many fail as leaders.

3. *Understand the American leadership preference.* Americans like reluctant leaders with a casual, easygoing style much more than pushy, formal ones. They like Tom Hanks in *Saving Private Ryan* or Jimmy Stewart going to Washington, not Gordon Gekko of "greed is good" fame.

4. *Honor moral leadership.* A lot has been made of values-based leadership in recent years, but even Attila the Hun had values. When people say values-based leadership, they tend to be implying they have the right values, therefore their position should be followed. I prefer to think about the moral base of leadership. Is your position on the side of the angels (consult your own God here)? Is it life affirming? How would it look on the front page of *The New York Times*? Does it feel right in your gut? And most important, what would your mother say?

5. *Lead the revolution.* Strategy guru Gary Hamel's book *Leading the Revolution* (Harvard Business School Press, 2000) is a must-read about the importance of breakthrough innovation in business strategy. Hamel in a nutshell, and in his own words:

> I found that most successful companies . . . were following the polestar of some truly noble aspiration. What counted was not so much how they positioned themselves against longstanding rivals, but how creatively they used their core competencies to create entirely new markets.

Health care desperately needs innovation, not just in process and tools but in business and organizational design. We need leaders who can imagine better futures.

Government-Run Health Care

*Powerful forces will expand public funding
of health care no matter what.*

About the time you read this we will have Government-Run Health Care. No, it's not what you think. While Obamacare has passed in Congress, the full effect of the legislation will not be felt until 2014 and beyond. No, what I mean is that even if health care reform is repealed, or blocked in implementation, the public-sector share of health spending will exceed 50 percent in 2010 for the first time.

Wait, you wonks say, the official CMS projections say that doesn't happen until 2012. (See "Health Spending Projections through 2019: The Recession's Impact Continues," by Christopher J. Truffer, Sean Keehan, Sheila Smith, Jonathan Cylus, Andrea Sisko, John A. Poisal, Joseph Lizonitz, and M. Kent Clemens, in *Health Affairs,* vol. 29, no. 3 [March/April 2010].) True, but read the fine print. That forecast assumes that Medicare follows current law and cuts Medicare physicians' fees by 20 percent in March because of the sustainable growth rate (SGR) provisions. Since SGR is set to get its annual stay of execution extended for another year, if you follow the authors' own math, then sometime in mid-2010 public payment will exceed private payment in American health care for the first time.

Demography and Recession

As the CMS projections show, this is a result of relentless demographic change, coupled to the lingering effects of the massive economic downturn, which raised Medicaid burdens by a record annual increase of 3.3 million eligibles (to a total of 46.3 million), swelled the ranks of the COBRA-subsidized, and reduced the total number of privately insured by 1.2 percent. But this is no short-term phenomenon. CMS's current law projection has the public sector growing more than the private sector as far as its eye can see (which is up until 2019). Beyond that, you don't need to be an actuary or futurist to realize that the private sector is unlikely to make a late-breaking comeback in the fourth quarter because of the aging of the baby boom. (By the way, one of my working definitions of a futurist is an actuary who doesn't like numbers.)

Remember, the Baby Boomers have just started to become Medicare eligible. We are on our way! We Boomers can't wait to convert from the uncertainty and capriciousness of private-sector health insurance coverage—especially those of us buying individual coverage from Anthem in California (as my family does)—and get our hands on one of those Magic Kingdom cards that is Medicare, which guarantee that we can see pretty much any doctor and that Medicare will at least pay them something. Sounds pretty good to me, even though the benefit consultants and financial planners tell us we also will each need to save $500,000 for our lifetime out-of-pocket medical costs not covered by Medicare. That still may be a better deal than a lifelong relationship with Anthem, trust me.

Higher Taxes Are Inevitable

Republicans are not the mean-spirited rubes that so many sneering progressive intellectuals make them out to be. They understand this math perfectly, and they do not want any part of the massive tax increases that this inexorable, demographically induced march implies.

Republicans were therefore not exactly big fans of the Obama administration wanting to expand coverage to the poor and middle class through government subsidies (albeit that the administration plans are in part financed by provider rate cuts in Medicare). Plus, all of the Democratic legislation expands Medicaid by 16 million enrollees. Medicaid is another publicly financed program, not particularly near and dear to the core Republican voter (or, as the polls show, it is not particularly popular with Independents).

The Republican Plan

So the demographic inevitability of higher taxes for health care motivates Republicans to fight any health care coverage expansion that is funded through public financing.

This partly explains what happened at the exquisite Kabuki Theater of the Health Care Summit at Blair House. The Republicans' goal was to stop this roller coaster; better yet, reverse it. Step 1 was to stop Obamacare. The Republicans had exactly the same cue cards—some Republican leaders read them better than others—but they all said: "Start over, clean sheet of paper, step by step." It could be a top-forty electro-pop lyric that would make the Black Eyed Peas proud.

Step 2 is to propose sensible, reasonable, American alternatives. (By the way, clue me in here, who gets to decide what are sensible, reasonable, American alternatives?)

The Republican plan was estimated to reduce the uninsured by 3 million, and this was achieved, as follows:

Say "free market" a lot. Government health care is bad, free-market health care is good. (I graduated from Edinburgh University 200 years to the day after Adam Smith went there to write *The Wealth of Nations*, and we still see each other at alumni meetings. He would be appalled that the term *free market* was applied to anything in American health care. Even private-sector health care bears little resemblance to a free market.)

Create high-risk pools at the state level so you can turbo-charge the death spiral in the insurance market. A high-risk pool makes health insurance cheaper for healthy people and more expensive for sick people. Whenever high-risk pools have been established at the state level, they rapidly death-spiral out of control.

Provide tiny wee tax credits for "affordable insurance." The polls show Americans like tax credits, particularly for small business. What the polls don't always measure is that the tax credits would not be sufficient to pay for the insurance; getting a tiny wee tax credit toward a very big expensive health insurance bill doesn't sound so good.

Create "affordable insurance policies" that don't cover anything. We know how to make health insurance premiums cheaper. It's simple: Limit what's covered and raise the cost sharing. But wait, isn't that what everyone's mad about?

Encourage consumers to buy "affordable insurance" from an insurance company in another state that has no consumer protection and no contractual relationship with local doctors and hospitals. Practically, insurance executives tell me, there really are no states with significantly cheaper policies that could be sold in other states, unless of course they are trying to eliminate consumer protection. Or maybe it's because of the bargaining clout that an insurer in Alabama has over my doctor in Palo Alto, California.

Reform malpractice caps to reduce defensive medicine, and let doctors focus on offensive medicine. Policy wonks dismiss malpractice as a driver of health care costs, but it is a big issue to doctors and to Republicans. (Personally, I believe the Obama administration missed a huge opportunity from the beginning by not embracing comprehensive medical malpractice coupled to patient safety reform.)

Increase personal responsibility. Successful surgeon-senators advocate for "skin in the game"; community organizer–presidents empathize more with $40,000-a-year families who can't pay for food or gas, let alone health insurance. These families have more than enough skin in the game.

Borrow more money from the Chinese so we can cut taxes. Deficits would remain large and growing even if all these "sensible, step by step" plans were pursued. Therefore, any tax cuts would have to be financed by borrowing from the Chinese, just as we have over the last decade.

The Democratic Plan

In the interest of being fair and balanced, we need to scrutinize the health reform legislation that just passed in Congress with the same degree of "vitriolic sardonicism," as Monty Python called it.

Democrats will cover 30-plus million of the uninsured (ten times the Republican number), and they achieve this as follows:

Expand Medicaid by 16 million because it is such a swell program. The Patient Protection and Affordable Care Act expands Medicaid by 16 million enrollees. When did Medicaid become such a great program? Did I miss a class? I thought it was horribly inefficient from an enrollment point of view and provided such pathetic levels of reimbursement that most mainstream providers won't accept Medicaid patients. Yet it has become the vehicle for half of the newly covered. Maybe that is why so many moderates liked the Wyden-Bennet proposal where people get a voucher. And there's your answer to why the Wyden-Bennet plan had no traction: It's pretty easy to stop printing little vouchers under a change in administration; it's a little more difficult to dismantle an entitlement program for 60 million people.

Have taxpayers in the states with generous Medicaid programs subsidize the Medicaid expansion in the states with less generous Medicaid. I spent the week of the Kabuki Summit, not in Washington, New York, or California, but in Oklahoma and South Dakota. And I heard about, and experienced directly, entire local state legislatures and majorities of individuals in the community committed to sending back Obamacare money to Washington if it passed, refusing to accept the rule of the federal government if reform passed, and pleas of "Liberty or death."

Whoa! The delicious irony is that the greatest potential beneficiaries of Obamacare are the very states with the most tight-fisted Medicaid programs. Liberal California software executives and closet lefty Goldman Sachs partners would be paying increased federal taxes to support the Medicaid programs for the less-than-munificent taxpayers of Texas and Alabama. The Massachusetts voters figured this out in their vote for Republican Scott Brown to the U.S. Senate; they already had Obamacare and like it, so why did they need to pay twice?

Mandate that most other uninsured Americans buy health insurance that they can't really afford. Under Obamacare you must have health insurance, unless you really can't afford it, or you work for a very small business (where most of the uninsured are), or you are a Christian Scientist, or you take a free ride because you can do first-grade arithmetic and figure out that paying the fine is way cheaper than buying insurance. Apart from those limited exceptions, you must have insurance.

And then subsidize them so they can. Did we tell you that we are subsidizing you to buy unaffordable insurance? (Ben Stein, the noted economist, columnist, and media celebrity, said on CNN after the summit that we should just give poor people the money to buy health insurance in the private market.) Here's the conversation you would have with a typical uninsured family with two kids, making $40,000 a year:

> "Hey folks. I am from the government. Here's $12,000, but we would like you to buy health insurance with it."
>
> "This is *Candid Camera*, right?"

Regulate insurance companies to take all comers even though all comers are not going to come. There is this pesky little problem with private health insurance markets. Insurers want to make sure that the people who sign up are not just sick people. And if they sign up only sick people, they want to be able to charge what it costs to treat those sick people, plus a fee for administration. Come on now. Be reasonable.

Raise fees and taxes on stakeholders who will pass them on in higher costs to the end consumer. Tax drug companies, medical device manufacturers, insurers and providers. These taxes will be passed on immediately to the end user in higher prices.

Start the taxes now; add the coverage later so in the next ten years it actually reduces the deficit. Gather in all the taxes now, so you can pay for expanded coverage later. If you have new revenues for a few years before the costs start, it is easier to make it budget neutral and in fact actually reduce the deficit. But . . .

In the long run, hold your breath and be prepared to borrow even more money from the Chinese. Once we get to a true run rate of the costs of reform, it may be difficult to say we are reducing the deficit because of reform.

We now know who really won the Kabuki Summit. Rahm Emanuel and the Democratic leaders in Congress have "persuaded" enough blue dog Democrats to vote for the good of the party for health reform with this parting comment:

"We know you are going to lose your seat over this, but you have to vote for this; otherwise we won't have health reform for another decade, and then it's too late. We're sorry it didn't work out for you here. But we have some parting gifts for you. Thanks for playing."

This is historic, important, and directionally correct legislation that will change health care dramatically when it is fully implemented in 2014. But even in the interim, we will have Government-Run Health Care no matter what. We just have to learn how to make it all work better.

Flip the Switch

Hospitals have to pick their tipping point.
And then act.

Health care reform is the new reality. All stakeholders are reading the fine print, and the tea leaves, and trying to identify what it all means. There are two big themes in the new law: First, more people will be covered but at lower reimbursement; second, there are seeds of change to shift the game from pay for procedures to pay for outcomes. All the rest is regulatory gobbledygook, aimed at making state insurance commissioners insane and giving the alternate universe that is Fox News something to be against.

How do hospitals prepare for these fundamental changes?

Fifteen years ago, I wrote a book called *The Second Curve: Managing the Velocity of Change* (Ballantine, 1996). It was an embarrassingly simple premise: Most businesses and most industries are going along quite nicely on their first curve (the base business, the business they know how to run on a daily basis). But they have a sneaking suspicion that it will be replaced by a second curve: a new business, or a new way of doing business, that is radically different from the first.

The dirty little secret of futurism is that you cannot predict the future, and there is a natural human tendency to overestimate the impact of phenomena in the short run and underestimate the impact in the long run. This causes multiple strategic errors: Companies jump too soon, walking away from all of the profit and revenue on the first curve; even more fatal, they cannot build the second curve, and they end up not making it in the long run as the forces of change make them irrelevant in a new world. Or worse yet, the second curve puts them in direct competition with themselves or their best customers. Oops, what to do?

The benefit of writing a book is that people who read it ask you to come and give a talk because they resonate to the premise. The bad part is that you get to meet people who have even better examples of what you wrote than the ones in the book, and it's too late to include them.

What I Know Now

I gave a few hundred Second Curve lectures to many, many companies in many, many industries and a lot of different countries over the last fifteen years. I learned four big lessons that I didn't fully appreciate when I wrote the book.

Americans love the frontier. Every group I talked to was eager to start the second curve. I used to recommend as a strategy that CEOs give $50 million in start-up money and a bunch of stock options to a bunch of crazy people in the organization to start the second curve. I thought it was an outrageous and provocative idea. Yet, in every session, there would be instant volunteers. Everyone wanted to be the future, even if it was risky, and even unlikely, and a little nuts.

Premature extrapolation. My old colleague Paul Saffo, the celebrated technology forecaster and master of the bon mot, once said: "Never confuse a clear view for a short distance." I redubbed that classic insight "premature extrapolation." Just because it is obviously going to happen doesn't mean it has to start immediately.

For example, in our work in the early 1990s for Pitney Bowes and the largest, most sophisticated postal services around the world, we built a forecast on the future of mail. Based on research, surveys, and countless expert panels, we developed a forecast that mail would eventually start to decline in use because the two main underpinnings of first-class mail (bills and statements on the one hand, direct marketing on the other) would migrate to electronic form. But our forecasts and scenarios also showed that in the United States, there was a high degree of attachment to paper-based mail in those two key areas.

We built careful monitoring systems with our clients so they could follow the true path of the first curve, even as they built the second curve. Mail in America grew slowly but steadily until 2007! If our clients had walked away from the first-class mail stream and bet the farm on the second curve too early, they would have walked away from nearly twenty years of steady, profitable growth.

Second curves take time to build. The key challenge of the second curve is that the business model is nearly always different from the first. But, most importantly, it involves a different culture, and cultural change does not happen quickly or easily. If you really want to have a different culture five years from now, you should have started a couple of decades ago. No kidding.

Most leaders can't deal with strategic schizophrenia. I was like Pollyanna when I wrote the book. I extolled people to manage on two curves. But I had precious few examples beyond IBM, which actually successfully managed the transitions from adding machines to mainframes, then mainframes to PCs, then PCs to the Internet, then the Internet to consulting services. Most organizations don't do well managing on two curves. Second-curve players (disruptive innovators, as Harvard's Clay Christensen calls them) are easy to find. But few know how to manage on two curves because the curves are so different; they have different cultures, people, heroes, and incentives.

Reimbursement Reform

So, back to hospitals.

Expansion of coverage, albeit at lower reimbursement, is something a hospital can handle, but reimbursement reform is a new game. The legislation includes important pilot programs to promote accountable care organizations (which take full financial risk for the care of patients) and to encourage bundled payment experiments (where the fee for the hospitalization would cover immediate pre- and post-discharge care as well as the associated physician fees and any risk of readmission). These are but the beginning of a long, inevitable path to changing the reimbursement system to reward value, not volume. We have only just begun.

The future, in the long run, may be very different: You have to prepare, and you must start now, because if you don't, you're toast.

But you will be in a world of strategic schizophrenia for some time to come.

Here's my best guess of what to do:

Integrate for accountable care. Take the building blocks of accountable care (financial risk for the care of patients, integrated medical staffs dedicated to high performance, performance measurement and management across the continuum of care, and a business model to sustain it all) and bring them together. Easy to say, hard to do. But this is your work.

Make care cheaper. Any way you cut it, making health care services cheaper will be a good thing. Cheap doesn't mean inferior or nasty. It means that it costs less. Like Wal-Mart with its superior, high-tech supply chain that delivers everyday low prices, hospitals that get ahead of the curves on aggressive cost management will be well ahead in any future.

Make care better. Be a maniac for measurement and performance improvement. You have to constantly strive to measure and improve, and everyone on your team needs to believe that, whether they work directly for you or not. Good morning, Doctor, let's chat.

Focus on outcomes. The bottom line of health care is great health outcomes for patients and populations—not profitable procedures, technically perfected for paying patients. Good outcomes may be death with dignity, or return to health status, or living well with chronic disease. Lose the scalpel; focus on the patients and the outcomes they want.

Innovate on the side. Successful second curves are built from pilots and experiments, often off to the side. For example, IBM's low-cost PC business was first built in isolation in Florida away from the dominant corporate culture. So, too, hospitals may have to pilot medical home initiatives and bundled payment experiments with small teams of innovators to learn how to play a new game.

Flip the switch. Constantly look to the future: Build the culture and capacity for the second curve as well as the business model for a different game while doing your best to nurture the organization that brought you into the millennium. But then, you, the leader, have to determine when to "flip the switch" and focus the entire organization on that new game. That's leadership.

The New Math

We need a new math for health care.
The old math isn't working.

It's becoming increasingly clear that the future of health care is now arithmetically impossible. You know—the future where the trend bends, the people get everything they want without paying more, the doctors are whole and happy, the hospitals flourish because there are no uninsured, and the ERs are empty because everyone has an insurance card and goes to her regular doctor instead.

Well, it was nice PowerPoint while it lasted. Reforming the health care insurance system without fundamentally changing the health care delivery system is mathematically impossible. We need a new math for the entire system.

Welcome to the Future under the Old Math

The old math is based on the notion that you pay providers every time they do something. Some patients have cards that pay providers a lot; some patients have cards that pay providers a little; some patients have no cards. The trick, if you are a hospital, is to have more patients with well-paying cards than patients with no cards. For a doctor, it is best to avoid the no-card patients entirely—unless you work for a federally qualified health center and you therefore get paid a lot per unit of service for the patients with no cards; or you are doctoring in a big safety net institution on a salary; or you are simply noble, hard working, and eager to be extremely badly compensated.

With health reform, some of the people with no cards will get cards that have poor reimbursement attached to them. (They are called Medicaid patients, and they will expand by 16 million under the law.) Doctors won't see these patients because the doctors are already too busy. Hospitals will see them, somewhat reluctantly, because they have no real choice. They will lose money on each of the patients, and they will try to make it up on volume, until they find they can't.

Then there are the people with the richly paying cards (who are employed by companies that currently offer health insurance at an annual cost of $18,000 a year in premium for a PPO family product). These companies are going to be the target of cost shifting by doctors and hospitals until the companies decide they have to move their employees' jobs to India because they can't afford to pay the money for cost-shifted health care. The unemployed patients will go on Medicaid or get substantial federal subsidies to purchase insurance through a federally subsidized health insurance exchange.

Everyone is grumpy, no one can afford the taxes, the premiums are ridiculous, hospitals cannot make money, and you have to wait forever to see a doctor. Doctors want to retire but they can't: Their 401(k) never recovers because health care costs are ruining the economy. This is not good.

A New Math for Health Care

All this misery is predicated on two key assumptions: first, that reimbursement should cover the costs of care; second, that the way we do things now is the right way.

I think we need a new math. When CFOs say to me that "Medicare covers only 95 percent of the costs of care," I rephrase that as "Medicare doesn't meet the current income expectations that your people have for delivering the service in exactly the same inefficient way as today." Doesn't sound so good.

Similarly, physicians who refuse to take Medicaid patients (most of them) and those who refuse to take Medicare patients (about 20 percent and growing) are basically saying the same thing: "You are not meeting my income expectations for me doing things the same way I have always done them."

Every business in every other industry has had to change what it does and how it does it. We need to learn from those businesses and industries about how to change.

But also, we need to help these providers out of the bind they are in by developing a New Math:

Population-based payment. Pay integrated systems of care a risk-adjusted, per capita fee to cover a population. (Wait, you say, that sounds like capitation! Dude, it is capitation. Get over it.) If these integrated systems of care can develop a way to deliver services that result in superior health outcomes for the population they cover, and the systems make money, God bless them, so long as there are performance scorecards and the patients join these systems voluntarily and willingly (with an incentive to select low-cost, high-performing systems).

Change the delivery model with technology. One doctor can see twenty patients per day. How many patient encounters per day can be generated by a team of one doctor, three nurse practitioners, five patient service representatives, and a big honking server? I don't know, but the fact that Kaiser had close to 9 million e-visits last year and took its in-person visits down to 60 percent of the prior year, by all accounts, speaks to a new math emerging in how to use technology to do more with the limited number of doctors we have.

Change the compensation principle from action to outcome. Patients want health outcomes, not health services. They can be encouraged to watchfully wait, rather than be aggressively treated. When pleasantly presented by persuasive professionals, patients pick properly. The shared-decision-making literature is full of lessons on how to do this if the incentives mesh with the decision-making science.

Pay doctors more (sometimes at the micro level) to save money at the macro level. It may be better to spend a well-compensated hour with a co-morbid congestive heart failure patient than to have that patient become part of the all-too-familiar "revolving door" of chronic care management in acute care hospitals. This will not happen spontaneously without a new math to support the economics of medical homes, accountable care organizations, and readmission reimbursement.

Release the power of pyramids. Referral pyramids can lead to volume-quality virtuous cycles. Similarly, delegation of tasks down the clinical pyramids can improve throughput and quality so that everyone is practicing at the limit of scope of practice, and those limits are being expanded through licensure, decision support, organizational innovation, and clinical redesign.

I am encouraged that if we are lucky and get good leadership from the Department of Health and Human Services and CMS and from the policy and academic communities, we can conceive of a new math that will lead us to a sustainable future. For example, I was really excited to learn that a friend and colleague, Dr. Arnie Milstein (who retains his role as chief medical officer of the Pacific Business Group on Health) will be leading the new Clinical Excellence Research Center at Stanford University. The center is dedicated to bringing engineering, business, and clinical faculty together to pursue innovation that will lead to high-performance health care delivery that is truly better, faster, and cheaper. I can't wait to see the fruits of that new effort.

But while theory, policy, pilots, and thought leadership are all important in developing a new math for health care, the most important critical success factor for the future is a health care field (and health care leaders) *willing to embrace* this new math. I believe that a new generation of health care leadership will come of age under the new math and that they'll figure it out, like it, work it, and create great health systems for the future. And then the math might work out for all of us.

On securing
our future

In Search of the
Next Economy

Will you still need me, will you still feed me,
when I'm sixty-four?

The global economic boom of the last quarter century got found out in the meltdown of the last two years. It was fun while it lasted, and it sustained unprecedented (some would argue wasteful and unnecessary) growth in the health care sector. The old global economy was predicated on Asian toil and savings subsidizing American self-indulgence, gluttony, and sloth. Bankers made out like bandits creating esoteric and highly lucrative instruments to facilitate the to-ing and fro-ing of cash. The rest of us just got older, fatter, and more stressed out as we worked too hard and then collapsed in an overleveraged heap.

Health care reaped the rewards of global growth by skimming an ever larger share off the top of corporate profits, government revenues, and household incomes. No one complained because we had houses and pickups and jet skis and Applebee's, and when we overindulged, we had fancy stents and well-heeled hospitals fixing our failing corpus. That game is so over.

Understanding the Global Economy before 2007 in Ten Easy Steps

I am not a card-carrying economist, but I know enough to be dangerous. Really smart people (whether true economists or not) have thought long and hard about what has happened in the global economy. (I particularly like the work of Harvard historian and fellow Glaswegian, Niall Ferguson, whose *Ascent of Money* was a wonderfully insightful review of recent economic history, especially his concept of Chimerica, the intricate codependence between American investment and consumption on the one hand and Chinese production and saving on the other.)

Drawing on the work of these smart people, here is my simple-minded take on how the global economy worked prior to the meltdown, in ten easy steps.

1. Hard-working people in communist countries (e.g., China, Vietnam) made good, cheap products and exported them to America at a profit.
2. They saved as much money as they could (like 30 percent of their income; before the meltdown, the U.S. savings rate was zero).
3. They loaned their money to U.S. banks and government.
4. Our banks leveraged the money 30-to-1 and loaned it to Americans to buy big houses we couldn't really afford.
5. Many Americans (and a lot of immigrants) were fully employed building these houses, cleaning them, and selling mortgages and title insurance.
6. Some Americans worked as nurses, doctors, teachers, waiters, or cooks because they weren't any good at real estate or construction.
7. The rest of Americans were prison guards or gave PowerPoint presentations to each other.
8. We all had jobs, we all could borrow money to buy stocks and more houses, and there was great demand, so the value of houses and stocks kept going up. And because we all felt rich . . .
9. We got to borrow even more money so that . . .
10. We filled our houses with good, cheap products made by hard-working people in Communist countries.

As we say in Glasgow, this is half joking, full serious. We have been on a consumption binge fueled by asset inflation. This binge was a product of cheap U.S. money and unrealistically loose credit, supported by artificially high Asian savings rates buoyed by artificially low foreign exchange rates. Add lack of government oversight and a global financial market that rewarded speculation, leverage, and trading over prudence, parsimony, and sustainability, and you have a recipe for financial disaster.

We know the story:

- $6 trillion of home equity wiped out since 2005 (along with all the hopes, dreams, and economic security that home equity represents);
- reduction in stock values to a new normal Dow at 10,000 with lackluster growth anticipated;
- national income growth stalled, personal income declining, and, in turn, government tax revenues at federal, state, and local levels in severe deficit;
- massive credit card balances for working families left unpaid or unpayable;
- lack of demand for goods and services, because working families can't afford Applebee's, nail salons, prescription drugs, doctors' visits, or elective surgery;
- serious European belt tightening because of those countries' own profligacy and government spending, further crimping global demand; and
- 14.6 million unemployed; millions more underemployed; and millions more with reduced work hours, furloughs, elimination of overtime, and, in an increasing number of cases, an absolute reduction in wages for those who have jobs.

The contraction of employment and the asset devaluation has touched almost everyone, from rich retirees to such highly trained professionals as lawyers, accountants, and techies, to teachers, firefighters, and the waitress at your local diner.

Health care was not unscathed in the economic meltdown. As we forecast in "Meltdown" (pp. 95–98), an essay published in the depth of despair in January 2009, health care did take significant hits in terms of patient volumes, Medicaid reimbursement rates, rising uninsured, increasing bad debt loads, and difficulty accessing capital. (Indeed, the latest figures just released for 2009 show that the number of uninsured grew by 4.4 million in 2009 to an astonishing 50.7 million. A full 7 million people lost their employment-related health insurance in 2009. Had it not been for expansions in Medicaid enrollment and the Children's Health Insurance Program, the total uninsured would have skyrocketed further. What is perhaps most alarming is that more than half of those who became uninsured in 2009 had annual household incomes of more than $50,000.)

Despite all this economic turmoil, total health care spending continued to grow, albeit more slowly, and employment in health care continued to grow continuously over the last year. From June 2009 to July 2010, according to the Bureau of Labor Statistics, health care employment grew by 231,000 jobs, from 13.54 million to 13.77 million. Hospitals alone added 35,000 jobs, one of the few bright spots in the whole economy.

The Obama administration deserves a lot of credit for avoiding the economic Armageddon that was perilously close. Despite the stimulus package, the happier news at General Motors, and the oil leak being capped, we are still a bit worried about the massive deficit and, more troubling to the average citizen, the lackluster job and income growth prospects as far as the eye can see. We are all in search of the Next Economy.

In Search of the Next Economy: The Global View

The Global Economy is not over, but it might be different in the future. Here are some ideas of how the Next Economy might work from a global perspective.

China and India grow up. If China were to allow its currency to strengthen and the Chinese consumed more at home, we might all be better off. For example, according to *The New York Times* on July 22, 2010:

> In the first half of this year, GM's sales in China rose 48.5 percent from a year earlier, and for the first time ever, the automaker sold more vehicles in China than in the United States. . . . GM sold nearly

half a million Buicks in China last year, almost five times the brand's sales in the United States.

Internal domestic consumption growth in China can make America better off. Similarly, the India market has huge opportunities to grow as its population surges past China in the decades ahead.

Europe smartens up. Europe is biting the bullet. From the PIGS (Portugal, Ireland, Greece, Spain) to the once business-like United Kingdom, the deficit issues are enormous. On a recent visit to Ireland, I witnessed the carnage of a burst bubble. While outwardly prosperous and perpetually cheerful, the Irish have been through an economic roller coaster that has seen deficits rise to a high of 14.3 percent of GDP in 2009, GDP fall by 7 percent in 2009, and property values decline by 30 percent. In Dublin's tony Merrion Square area, every second elegant Georgian doorway has a To Let (For Lease) sign, and the brass plaques of the former tenants portray a cadre of hedge fund managers, property speculators, and assorted economic hangers-on, vaporized as the bubble burst. (I should say that Ireland still has extraordinarily expensive real estate; a modest little bungalow in the suburbs of Dublin might list at 1.5 million euros!) While growth is now essentially flat in 2010, the Irish remain cheerful, charming, and convinced of happier times ahead, but they are in a very deep hole, with total debt at 997 percent of GNP in 2009 compared with the United Kingdom at 409 percent; United States, 93 percent; Canada, 62 percent; India, 20 percent; and China, 7 percent.

Throughout Europe, governments (including the recently elected Conservative–Liberal Democrat coalition government in the United Kingdom) are tackling their deficits by raising taxes and cutting public spending and by taking really tough steps for Europeans (including reducing public pension schemes, cutting services, and pairing back public-sector employment). If the French are taking on pension entitlements, you know it's serious! The trick will be not to overdo it and contribute to a worldwide, double-dip Grand Recession. In the long run, generous health and pension costs will have to be paid through the toil and taxes of young immigrants from within the European borders and beyond, who will be needed to sustain economic growth in the European Union.

Africa wakes up. Following a superbly organized World Cup, South Africa was seen by the world as a modern, sophisticated nation. The whole of Africa may have an opportunity to come into its own in the next two decades and climb out of the postcolonial malaise of corruption, political and tribal infighting, and crushing poverty and disease. What if China chose to subsidize African growth and consumption instead of American, in exchange for access to Africa's natural resources? What would the global economy of 2050 look like? We might find out in the decades ahead.

Latin America turns up. The Latin American miracle is that it has not collapsed in its last fifty years of economic turmoil. Progress is being made through a weird combination of petro-socialism (such as Venezuela), narco-autocracy (as in Colombia), and good old-fashioned industrialization (Brazil and Argentina). A growing middle-class market and a lot of natural resources make all of Latin America another natural target for Asian investment and economic partnership.

Islam wants up. There are about a billion Muslims in the world, and most live in economically repressed nations. Some citizens, like the Saudis and Kuwaitis, get bought off by their oil-rich leaders, while migrant workers from Pakistan do all the hard work. Other Islamic countries—Iraq and Afghanistan come to mind—struggle economically and remain horrible examples of corruption, inequity, and inefficiency. Countries like Turkey (not without its own problems), which is secular in government and mostly Islamic in the private lives of its citizens, represents, perhaps, the best possible example of how Islamic nations can embrace freedom, democracy, and markets without losing face or faith.

The United States 'fesses up. And we in the United States, yes, we need to 'fess up. We need to admit that lower taxes mean higher deficits. And that Proposition 13–like tax provisions and the tax deductibility of mortgage interest may be great for individuals, but as a society they are luxuries we cannot afford. And that most government spending at the state and local levels goes to health care for the poor, education, and prisons, and no one wants to cut these programs. But that, in turn, generous public-sector pensions and health benefits for workers in those sectors are unsustainable. And finally, that rising health care costs are the primary threat to long-term budget deficits, not because of more old people or more poor people or more covered people under Obamacare, but because of the continuously rising intensity, and thus costs, of medical services for people in public programs. And before you say: "Well, shift them to private programs," the problem is that private programs are even more costly, and most people can't pay for them, anyway; it's all too expensive, and most of us need a subsidy. Unless we change the way we do what we do.

In Search of the Next Economy: The U.S. View

Look, it's really not that bad. I believe in the United States and the energy and ability of its people to create a better life. I also believe that the Chinese, the Indians, the Brazilians, the Russians, the Turks, and the Estonians want that, too, if you give them half a chance. It will all work out in the end. Trust me.

Let me offer one view of how the U.S. economy may reshape itself over the next decade and what it means for health care. The economy may be composed of a number of different sectors:

The ultra-productive, high-performing, globally competitive economic base. There is emerging a high-performing, ultra-productive economic base in the United States that takes ideas, knowledge, innovation, branding, marketing, and technology and turns them into profits on a global basis. Think Microsoft, Oracle, Google, Apple, Intel, Cisco, and Salesforce.com, but also think P&G, Coca-Cola, Johnson & Johnson, Amgen, and Pfizer. Along the way, they create a lot of profit but few jobs, as most of these high fliers manage global webs of production and distribution, and we consumers could care less where our iPad is made as long as Steve Jobs and his friends designed it. These companies primarily create profit and wealth, not jobs and incomes.

The new free-basing experience economy sector. Joe Pine and Jim Gilmore coined the term *the experience economy* a decade ago and wrote a great book about it. But a new variant is emerging based on a free base, as Chris Anderson (formerly of *Wired* magazine) artfully predicted.

For example, Facebook has more than 600 million members. It is privately held, but if it IPOs, as it might in the next year, its market cap could be stratospheric. Does it make money? Who knows? Who cares? But with 600 million users spending endless hours a day saying "Wassup?" to each other, it has to be worth a lot. It employs a few hundred people and occupies a few hundred million more.

Another good example is a start-up company called Bleacher Report, for which my son works in San Francisco. It is a sports fan–based website. Fans create content for free: Wannabee sports journalists lying on their couches in Wisconsin work very hard writing articles and creating other content. They do it for nothing more than exposure. Bleacher Report gets upward of 20 million unique visitors a month, and it is now in the top 100 Web sites on the planet. It does have employees, real offices, smart engineers, and server contracts all paid for by venture investors and, increasingly, by advertisers. Like most Silicon Valley start-ups, much of its office technology infrastructure is free: Google docs, Gmail, Gchat, and the like. The good news for health care is that, like most Silicon Valley start-ups, the company offers generous health benefits; the bad news for health care is that virtually no one in the company is older than thirty, and there are only two girls.

But the best example of this new free-base experience economy is Zynga. It makes games for Facebook and gives them away free. For instance, according to *The New York Times* on July 24, 2010:

> In FarmVille, its most popular game, players tend to virtual farms, planting and harvesting crops, and turning little plots of land into ever more sophisticated or idyllic cyberfarms. Good farmers—those who don't let crops wither—earn virtual currency they can use for things like more seed or farm animals and equipment. But players can also buy those goods with credit cards, PayPal accounts or Facebook's new payment system, called Credits. A pink tractor, a FarmVille favorite, costs about $3.50, and fuel to power it is 60 cents. A Breton horse can be had for $4.40, and four chickens for $5.60. The sums are small, but add up quickly when multiplied by millions of users: Zynga says it has been profitable since shortly after its founding.

You think I am kidding, right? People buy virtual chickens and tractors with real money so they can play a game on Facebook.

Zynga has 1,500 employees, up from 375 two years ago, and 400 current job openings. The company has been valued at $6.5 billion and has the backing of such Silicon Valley venture-elite companies as Kleiner Perkins Caufield & Byers.

Maybe there is an opportunity to provide virtual health care to virtual farmers?

Market-based meritocratic Maslowian economy. Most Americans will work in a market system of exchange, meeting basic needs through labor. The more you make, the higher up the Maslowian needs pyramid you will get. It will be meritocratic based on value creation, which, in turn, largely will be dependent on education levels. For example, in the depth of the recession, H1 visa slots available for engineers from abroad with bachelor's degrees remained unfilled because there was no demand, whereas master's degree-level requests for visas were oversubscribed. Folks will be working tables at Applebee's serving other folks who work tables at Applebee's, where they likely will be paid more in the form of health benefits than they earn in the form of wages. Smart bankers still will be buying big boats if they have really added value to companies and to shareholders. But they will be taxed more progressively, as the tax cuts expire, to pay for health and education programs for those who want to work their way out of waiting tables, and for the health programs of those who remain through choice or circumstance.

Gigantic Keynesian sector. The health care, education, and criminal justice systems represent a gigantic Keynesian sector that employs large numbers of people mostly supported by federal, state, and local taxes. These sectors will offer solid, though not spectacular, employment opportunities, shielded as they are from the worst sting of global competition by virtue of the fact that they are geographically bound social services. But in the future, employees of the organizations will have more modest pensions, skinnier health benefits, less overtime, and lower income growth, though they will have more economic security than most.

Freelancers. Liberated from job-lock, working forever to pay the bills, and forced out by restructuring and realignment in corporate America, armies of Baby Boomers will drift through the next decade eventually into Medicare but buying health benefits through insurance exchanges on the way. The individual market for health insurance purchased through exchanges will grow much more if employers decide to exit health benefits and send the employees to the insurance exchanges. It is unlikely to happen immediately, but a decade from now the scenario could be very different. For example, assume health insurance exchanges get established properly and work effectively from 2014 on. Assume further that the Cadillac tax comes into force in 2018 as planned, providing a major incentive for employers to opt out. Under these assumptions, and if employers feel morally freed to send their employees to the exchange (with some more generous employers giving employees a cash inducement, but other less generous employers giving employees simply an apology), then many employers may exit health benefits altogether, creating a massive shift to those plans sold through the exchanges.

The luxury sector. There still will be basketball stars, entrepreneurs, wealthy families, and smart lawyers who live in luxury. It won't be as good as the Bush years, but it still will be good to be rich. No matter what happens to the overall economy, there will be a lot of rich people in the United States (many of them non-U.S. citizens), and they will want and demand the best possible health care that money can buy. Problem is, there are not enough of them to go around, so competition for the luxury set will be fierce.

Change Or . . .

It might all sound a bit depressing, and it is certainly more austere. But it could turn out to be a bit fairer, more meritocratic, less capricious, and more sustainable than the economic boom we went through.

If health care leaders think they can survive and thrive in the decade ahead by focusing solely on the privately insured, then you have to ask: Where exactly are those privately insured going to come from in the Next Economy? And how rich will their insurance coverage be?

No matter what, health care leaders need to prepare for the Next Economy by making their health systems high performers: delivering superior quality at competitive costs. Health systems must also learn to survive and thrive on public payment levels and competitive, private-sector pricing and, most importantly, change how they deliver care. Do that and you still will be in the phone book in 2050 (at least on my iPad), and I will friend you on Facebook.

Chasing Unicorns:
The Future of ACOs

We have a great idea, a lot of momentum,
and no clue what might happen next.

My good friend and colleague Mark Smith, MD, MBA, president and CEO of the California Healthcare Foundation (on whose board I sit), said it best: "The accountable care organization is like a unicorn, a fantastic creature that is vested with mythical powers. But no one has actually seen one."

I have re-blogged and re-tweeted (twitter@seccurve) this so often that I received all the credit for the line. Welcome to the Internet age. But in all fairness to me, re-tweeting someone else's intellectual property is as close as most of us get to original thought these days.

And that, my friends, brings me to why chasing unicorns is so important. The rising cost of health care is a national security threat greater than any other. It will kill the budget; the economy; and, some even argue, the patients because of unaffordability, excessive iatrogenic interventions, and profligate use of resources. We desperately need some big new ideas about how to practically meet Don Berwick's noble triple aim of better care, better population health, and lower per capita costs.

One of those big new ideas is the accountable care organization, or ACO.

Well, actually it is not an entirely new idea. And many in health care can (and do) legitimately claim to having been one for a long time. Kaiser, Geisinger, Mayo, Cleveland Clinic, capitated delegated medical groups of California, and even a few network model HMOs, among others, can say they were doing this all along.

I gave a little after-dinner talk to an elite group of ACO thought leaders in Los Angeles (basically, the talk is the rest of this essay), and it was a combination of both a roast and an homage to Dr. Eliot Fisher of Dartmouth (who was there, I may add) and whom I always describe as a national treasure, not only for leading the wonderful *Dartmouth Atlas* work, which in many ways was the intellectual underpinning of, and the compelling case for, meaningful health reform, but also for being widely credited with coining the term *accountable care organization*. But, as Eliot would be the first to modestly admit, many others in the room that night (Enthoven, Shortell, Levine, Crosson, Margolis, O'Kane, Robinson, and too many more to acknowledge adequately here) are all part of the intellectual and practical foundations of this re-emergence of the accountable care organization vernacular.

At their very best, ACOs could be a powerful, successful re-tweet of Enthoven's managed competition, which a lot of us thought was a pretty decent American compromise the first time around (see my essay entitled "The New American Compromise," pp. 91–94). At its worst, it could be a badly defined mish-mash of half-baked ideas and experiments that is an orgy of excess for lawyers and consultants. As one colleague noted to me, probably half of the 1,500 attendees at the 2010 ACO Congress in Los Angeles were lawyers and consultants (including me) eager to arm themselves with a new PowerPoint for an assault on the dazed and confused delivery system. (Do a Google search for "ACO video" and you will find a brilliant cartoon about this on YouTube.)

So, here's my take on ACOs and what we have to do to make them work. I frame my suggestions simply and modestly, first as a central two-part problem, and second as Morrison's Ten Laws. (When you are a futurist, you're allowed to make up your own laws.)

The Mutual Disrespect Problem

There is in American health care a central problem governing the organization of health care. I call it the mutual disrespect problem, and it has two important parts:

Part 1: Everyone thinks everyone else's job is easy.
Part 2: Anyone can do what a health insurance company does.

There is in health care an astonishing degree of mutual contempt for the component parts of the system: Doctors hate hospital administrators, nurses hate doctors, and everyone hates insurance companies, especially the patients and the government.

Which brings me to the second part, namely, that every stakeholder assumes that whatever insurance companies do, the stakeholder could do easily for itself. I have written before that insurers will be asked to explain their own benefit to society (see my essay "Explanation of Benefits," pp. 58–60). Insurers are having an exceptionally profitable year through no particular genius on their part, it seems to me (just check their earnings against estimates). Despite all that, they actually do things that other actors (particularly hospitals and doctors) are pathetic at or incapable of, such as eligibility monitoring, enrollment management; administration of benefits; and, some would say, predictive modeling, population health management, case management, technology assessment, and, of course, risk management.

So it is important, before we embark on this path to accountable care, that we all start with a little self-awareness and good old-fashioned humility about core competencies to manage the risk for and outcomes of care for a defined population.

And so, to the Ten Laws.

Morrison's Ten Laws of Accountable Care

Morrison's First Law

Any organization that claims to be an accountable care organization probably:

- *is not accountable for a defined population*
- *doesn't care for patients beyond a few isolated episodes*
- *is not very well organized*

With the obvious exception of the organizations mentioned in this essay's introduction that have a legitimate historic claim to being proto-ACOs, most people who are announcing their institution as an accountable care organization are full of it. Indeed, sometimes the louder the claim, the weaker the evidence. (It's a bit like national politics, no?)

Morrison's Second Law

You can't be accountable for the care of patients . . . unless you know their phone numbers.

The way the ACO provisions are currently framed, patients who end up in an ACO will be assigned to it on the basis of an "attribution logic." Personally, if I were running an ACO, I'd rather know patients' phone numbers so I can call them up and harass them about what they are eating. If I am going to be accountable for their health expenses, then I would like to be a wee bit proactive about identifying and managing the risk. And a really good start would be to know exactly who the patients are. By the way, most doctors (or hospitals for that matter) don't have a clue as to what other providers their patients see or what their patients are doing when they are not with them, so this is not a new problem. It is just that now there will be money attached, both positively and negatively.

Morrison's Third Law

Patients in accountable care organizations should at least know they are in them.

Even I, with my perverted sense of humor, could not make this up. Patients in ACOs will not know they are in them. Mercifully, the policymakers are onto this aberration, so expect amended regulations that will require notifying the patients, possibly as follows:

> Dear Madam, Sir, or Occupant:
>
> Congratulations! Our attribution logic engine has automatically assigned you to get (almost all of) your health care from an organization with a new name that doesn't mean anything, but that actually used to be known as your local hospital. It is called an accountable care organization now, and it will be great for your health.
>
> Have a wonderful day.
>
> The People at Medicare
>
> P.S. They don't know who you are either, so you might want to give them a ring.

Morrison's Fourth Law

Patients in accountable care organizations should not be allowed to leave just because they had a bad day.

Under pressure from the freedom and liberty folks, no one had the juice to say that patients in ACOs have to stay with them. No, the patients can skate away whenever they like. Imagine the money-losing, noncompliant, frequent-flyer, congestive heart failure patient being dumped on your doorstep because the hospital a few miles away paid for the limo and subsidized the patient's rent so he or she could move in next door. Extreme, you say? In twenty-five years of observing American health care, I can say that it is a lot easier to dodge risk than manage care. This one really worries me, and I think it needs to be fixed through voluntary enrollment for one-, two-, or three-year periods; once you pick, you stay. This could end up being an ideological deal breaker.

Morrison's Fifth Law

Accountable care organizations must "bend the trend"; otherwise, it is a massive distraction for busy professionals who don't have a life already.

Look, everyone is busy. So unless we are prepared to get behind the notion of bending the costs curve through more accountable health delivery systems, it will be a massive distraction that diverts our attention from simpler, more immediate end points of improvement like avoidable readmissions, medication errors, or primary care redesign. We must commit to slowing if not reversing total costs growth.

Morrison's Sixth Law

Doctors love fee for service. They just want more fee and less service.

We policy wonks (especially the economists) love to talk about reimbursement reform: Change the incentives and the system will reform itself. We are always talking about the incentives for doctors (since their decisions drive most health care costs). So my colleagues at Harris Interactive had the brilliant idea of asking doctors how they feel about all that. The Harris surveys show that the majority of physicians are, on balance, somewhat satisfied with their current reimbursement method (namely, fee for service). They just complain about the amount of the payment for the level of effort involved in providing the service. But when it comes to changing the method of payment, the same surveys show that physicians don't seem to like any of the provider-payment reform ideas now circulating, including pay-for-performance schemes, bundled payment, or global episodic payment. A recent academic survey confirmed Harris's numbers that only about 16 percent of doctors would be in favor of accepting bundled payment.

The wonks designing bundled payment have not quite thought through the likely bloody wars in every hospital when a sack of money is dumped on the desk to cover all the costs of a hip or knee replacement: the diagnostic workup, the DRG payment, the surgeon's fee, the rehab, and the readmission risk. Fights over who gets what will be reminiscent of the second battle in *Braveheart*.

Morrison's Seventh Law

Any successful payment reform requires that you buy the doctors off in the short run so you can "grind the bastards down" in the long run.

This is an almost direct quote (including the profanity) of a prominent executive of the British National Health Service (NHS) when I asked her why it had spent 30 percent net new money on the British Primary Care Pay for Performance scheme. Generations before, Aneurin Bevan, father of the British NHS, was asked how in 1948 he secured the cooperation of the British doctors in health reform; he reputedly said: "I stuffed their mouths with gold."

A similar story could be told of the dawn of Canada's medical insurance in Saskatchewan in the 1960s. And yet, we in the United States did not learn the lesson of history, so the doctors never got a permanent sustainable growth rate fix in health reform (and still don't) going into a "spend no more" Congress. Oops.

Morrison's Eighth Law

One man's waste is another man's income.

There is enormous waste in American health care: unnecessary care, redundant care, defensive care, inappropriate care, unethical care, excessive care, futile care, and corrupt care. But one man's waste is another man's income. In Japan, they call waste *muda*. In Oklahoma, they call it margin. Extracting waste, at least in the short run, means someone's income either has to go down or disappear entirely; in the long run, we can reallocate. Again, this is easy to say, hard to do.

Morrison's Ninth Law

The high-value ACOs seen through a Medicare lens may not be high value seen through an all-payer lens. (In other words, if hospitals integrate locally to be accountable, will they end up being market dominating?)

There are really two important consequences of this law. First, despite the great work of the *Dartmouth Atlas,* it doesn't tell the whole story about performance—because to date the data have been Medicare only. Yet as I have written before (see my essay entitled "If Bernie Madoff Ran Health Care," pp. 9–13), because of the enormous variation in commercial insurance prices to providers in various parts of the country relative to Medicare, the hospitals and regions who show well or badly under Medicare numbers may not be as good (for example, Sacramento) or as bad (say, McAllen, Texas) as their Medicare-only *Dartmouth Atlas* shows. The easy solution is for Dartmouth to get an enormous grant from someone to put all the data together; to report it; and to let the boards of hospitals truly be accountable for analyzing, explaining, and governing their stewardship of resources.

The second idea in this law, and one that regulators are confronting head on and fast, is that if health care providers consolidate locally in the name of accountable care organizations, will it lead to a concentration of market power and, in turn, even higher prices? Provider consolidation has been going on like crazy for a decade, and many argue that this explains the rising prices seen in many markets. The ACO trend could make this situation even worse without appropriate policy and regulatory oversight.

Morrison's Tenth Law

The people most capable of managing the care of populations are the people least trusted to do it.

Certain, if not many, aspects of managing the care of populations may be done best by a managed care organization. Yet surveys of doctors and the public reveal that managed care organizations are the least trusted, are the most deserving of more regulations, and are perceived by physicians to have done more to harm quality than almost any stakeholder, with the exception of malpractice lawyers and the government.

Looking Ahead

Despite my natural Scottish cynicism, I am incredibly excited that the health care marketplace is embracing accountable care and that hospitals, in particular, are running as fast as they can to integrate with their physicians and figure out mutually beneficial ways to get higher performance for the communities they serve.

We should be deeply grateful to the leaders of the accountable care movement (past, present, and future) for their tireless efforts to energize the health care field to achieve better health for populations, higher quality of care, and lower cost. We salute you all.

Accountable care organizations are vaguely defined, conceptually fuzzy, and badly constructed, both legislatively and managerially, and they are potentially, profoundly unpopular with doctors and patients. But they may be our best hope to have an organized health care system that is accountable for our care.

Index